German Humanism

Twayne's World Authors Series

Ulrich Weisstein, Editor of German Literature

Indiana University

TWAS 690

OBSCVRI VIRI

Epiſtole Obſcurorū virorū ad Magiſtrū Ortuinū
Bratiū Dauentrienſem Colonie latinas litteras pro
ſirentē nō illę q̃ dē veteres et prius viſæ: ſed et nouę et illis prioribȝ
Elegantia argutijs lepore ac venuſtate longe ſuperiores.
Ad Lectorem.
Riſum Deraclitæ eſt: vaſti ridere parati
Arida murarū pectora Stoicidæ
Da mihi triſtem animū: ferales obſſ ce luctus
Diſperaã niſi moȝ omnia Riſus erunt.
Eȝerce pulmonem.

Woodcut from the first edition of the second
part of *The Letters of Obscure Men* (1517)

German Humanism

By Eckhard Bernstein

College of the Holy Cross

Twayne Publishers • Boston

German Humanism

Eckhard Bernstein

Copyright © 1983 by G. K. Hall & Company
All Rights Reserved
Published by Twayne Publishers
A Division of G. K. Hall & Company
70 Lincoln Street
Boston, Massachusetts 02111

Book Production by Marne B. Sultz

Book Design by Barbara Anderson

Printed on permanent/durable acid-free
paper and bound in the United States of
America.

Library of Congress Cataloging in Publication Data

Bernstein, Eckhard.
   German humanism.

   (Twayne's world authors series; TWAS 690)
   Bibliography: p. 156
   Includes index.
   1. German literature—Early modern, 1500–1700
—History and criticism.   2. Humanism in literature.
I. Title. II. Series.
PT251.B46 1983   830'.9'003   82–23324
ISBN 0–8057–6537–9

Contents

About the Author

Eckhard Bernstein is Professor of German at the College of the Holy Cross, Worcester, Massachusetts. He grew up in Saxony, East Germany, went to West Germany as a child in 1950 and to the United States in 1965. He studied at the Philipps-Universität Marburg, Germany, Exeter University, England, and received the Ph.D. in Comparative Literature from Case Western Reserve University, Cleveland, in 1972. Prior to his appointment at Holy Cross, he taught at Youngstown University and Lake Erie College.

In addition to publishing numerous book reviews in scholarly journals and a number of articles that appeared in *Daphnis, Classical Folia,* and *Die Unterrichtspraxis,* he has published two books, both in German. The first, entitled *Die erste deutsche Aeneis* (1974), is an analysis of Thomas Murner's translation of the *Aeneid* of 1515, the second, called *Die Literatur des deutschen Frühhumanismus* (Metzler, 1978) is an introduction to early German Renaissance literature, primarily dealing with the period between 1450 and 1480.

Preface

In a recent book, two French scholars offered the following assessment of German Humanism: "After the age of Goethe and the Weimar culture (or possibly that of the present time), German Humanism represents the third highpoint of German culture. Chronologically, it was the first major contribution of the German-speaking countries to a universal culture."[1] Since this flattering appraisal comes from an impeccably nonpatriotic source, we can be reasonably sure that it was not prompted by chauvinistic pride in the German past but by sound scholarship and a comparison with other manifestations of this international movement.

In its homeland, German Humanism has by no means fared as well. This has to do with the structure of the German universities as well as with the course of German intellectual history in the last two hundred years. Placed between the powerful *Altgermanistik* with its stress on old Germanic philology and medieval language and literature on the one hand, and the *Neugermanistik,* which only starts with the Baroque or even later, on the other, the literature of the fifteenth and sixteenth centuries, to which Humanism belongs, is a field for which nobody really feels responsible. As a result, very few university chairs have been designated for research in this area.

The other, possibly more important reason for its comparative neglect lies in the nature of German Humanism itself. Since most German Humanists wrote in Latin, their works were often regarded as something foreign and imitative by scholars who had been brought up in the tradition of German Romanticism which required a work of art to be indigenous and original.

This, of course, does not mean that no research was done. Nineteenth-century philologists have provided us with masterful editions of the works and letters of the major writers of the period. But it is also true that, in comparison with other periods of German literature, there are noticeable gaps. And although in recent years a great number of specialized studies have appeared, which prompted one German scholar to declare that "the former stepchild has become the favorite child of the scholars" (Wuttke), it is also a fact that many problems remain unsolved and many questions unanswered.

The object of this book is to introduce the American reader to the principal authors of German Humanism, the educational and cultural movement that extended from approximately 1450 to 1530. This is a difficult but challenging task. Humanism, like Romanticism, affected virtually all aspects of life. Thus it would, in principle, have been necessary to include the rich so-called *artes*-literature, that is, works on botany, geography, astronomy, astrology, mathematics, music, art, and magic. This was not done since it would far transcend the scope of the present book. The exclusion of these fields also meant that such important figures as Georg Peuerbach, Johannes Regiomontanus, Nicolaus Copernikus, Georg Agricola, and Theophrastus Paracelsus had to be omitted. Included are works of literature, understood not in the narrow sense of fiction and poetry but in the wider sense of all works written in what we now call the humanities, i.e., poetry, essays, treatises, historical, philosophical, and pedagogical works, satires, biographies, and letters, which were developed to an art form by the Humanists.

All translations from Latin and German into English are my own unless otherwise noted. An attempt was made to translate the Latin and German poems in their original meters. I daresay that I have reasonably succeeded only in the rendering of the *Knittelvers,* or doggerel, where the awkwardness of the translation is matched by the clumsiness of the original. Otherwise the reader has to judge for himself whether this attempt was worth the intellectual effort.

The Bibliography lists those books to which reference is made in the course of the book. That it is highly selective needs neither explanation nor apology. The field of German Humanism is so vast that a volume of this size could easily be filled with a bibliography of that movement alone—and even that would still be selective. To increase the usefulness for the American reader, English titles have been given preference wherever possible, although the standard works on individual Humanists, except Erasmus, are all written in German. In some cases, where other TWAS volumes have already appeared or are in preparation, the Bibliography has been kept to a minimum.

Finally, I am grateful to Professors William Zwiebel, my colleague at Holy Cross, and Ulrich Weisstein of Indiana University, the German editor of this series, for reading the entire manuscript and offering many valuable stylistic suggestions. I also would like to convey my sincere gratitude to the College of the Holy Cross for awarding me a Faculty Fellowship in the spring of 1980 and for generously supporting me with various smaller research grants during the writing of this book.

Eckhard Bernstein

College of the Holy Cross

Chronology

1453	Constantinople conquered by the Turks.
1455–1522	Johannes Reuchlin.
1456	Peter Luder delivers seminal inaugural address on the *studia humanitatis* in Heidelberg.
1457–1521	Sebastian Brant.
1457	Enea Silvio Piccolomini writes his *Germania*.
1459	Albrecht von Eyb completes his *Margarita poetica* (printed in 1472), a collection of excerpts from Roman, patristic, and Humanist literature.
1459–1508	Conrad Celtis.
1460	University of Basel founded.
1461	Niclas von Wyle begins to publish individual translations. Heinrich Steinhöwel's translation of the *Griseldis*.
1466/69–1536	Erasmus of Rotterdam.
1470–1526	Conradus Mutianus Rufus.
1472	Eyb's *Ehebüchlein*.
1472–1530	Willibald Pirckheimer.
1473–1474	Rudolf Agricola composes his *Vita Petrarchae*.
1473	Steinhöwel's *Von den synnrychen erluchten wyben*.
1474	Eyb completes *Spiegel der Sitten* (first printed 1511).
1476–1477	Steinhöwel's *Aesopus*.
1478	Wyle's *Tütschungen*.
1479	Rudolf Agricola finishes his *De inventione dialectica* (first printed 1518).
1480	Wimpfeling's *Stylpho*, first Humanist comedy, performed.
1484	Agricola writes a letter to a friend, which is later published under the title *De formando studio*.
1486	Celtis's *Ars versificandi*.
1487	Celtis crowned poet laureate by Emperor Frederick III.
1483–1546	Martin Luther.
1488–1523	Ulrich von Hutten.

1492   Celtis delivers his inaugural address, "the manifesto of German Humanism," at the University of Ingolstadt.

1493   Frederick III dies. Maximilian I crowned German Emperor. Celtis presents a manuscript of his *Norimberga* to the city council of Nuremberg.

1494   Sebastian Brant's *Narrenschiff* and Reuchlin's *De verbo mirifico* published.

1497   Reuchlin's drama *Henno* performed.

1497–1560   Philipp Melanchthon.

1499   As the result of the Swiss War, the Swiss Confederation gains de facto independence from the Empire.

1500   First edition of Erasmus's *Adagia*; Wimpfeling's *Adolescentia*.

1500–1574   Joachim Camerarius.

1502   Celtis's *Quattuor libri amorum*.

1503   Erasmus's *Enchiridion militis christiani*.

1505   Wimpfeling completes his *Epitome Rerum Germanicarum*.

1506   Reuchlin's *De rudimentis hebraicis*, the first Hebrew grammar and dictionary written by a Christian scholar.

1507–1509   Johannes Pfefferkorn in four books denounces the Jews.

1509   Erasmus publishes his *Encomium moriae {Praise of folly}*.

1510   Reuchlin's *Gutachten* ("legal opinion") concerning Hebrew books. Wimpfeling's pamphlet against Locher, defending theology and attacking poetry.

1511   Reuchlin issues his *Augenspiegel*.

1513   Giovanni de Medici becomes Pope Leo X. Celtis's *Odes* published posthumously.

1515–1517   *Epistolae obscurorum virorum* published anonymously.

1516 Erasmus edits his Greek New Testament, "the greatest scholarly achievement of German Humanism."

1517 Reuchlin's *De arte cabbalistica*. Luther nails his ninety-five theses against the sale of indulgences on the doors of the Schlosskirche in Wittenberg. Beginning of Reformation.

1518 At the Diet of Augsburg Luther refuses to recant.

1519 Maximilian dies. Charles V elected Emperor. In Leipzig Eck, Karlstadt, and Luther debate theological questions. The first edition of Erasmus's *Colloquia familiaria* appears.

1520 Hutten writes four dialogues denouncing Rome. Luther publishes four pamphlets against the papacy.

1521 Philipp Melanchthon has his *Loci communes* printed, the first systematic description of Protestant theology. Hutten's *Gesprächbüchlein* appears. The Diet of Worms convenes for the purpose of examining and passing judgment on the religious doctrines of Luther. The latter refuses to recant.

1522 Luther's German translation of the New Testament. Pirckheimer's *Laus Podagrae*.

1524–1525 Controversy between Erasmus and Luther on the "free and enslaved will." In a number of uprisings the German peasants try to improve their wretched conditions. They are defeated.

1528 Melanchthon issues his guidelines for school visitations in Saxony. Pirckheimer finishes the final draft of his *Bellum Helveticum*.

1530 Diet of Augsburg. Melanchthon drafts the *Augsburg Confession*, the chief statement of faith of the Lutheran Church.

Chapter One
Introduction

The term *Humanism* has acquired many different and divergent meanings in our century. Psychologists employ it as well as educators and philosophers; Christians lay claim to the term but so do Marxists. The eminent Renaissance historian Lewis W. Spitz diagnosed the situation clearly when he said in 1963 ". . . the historian will very shortly have to reckon with as many humanisms as there have been French republics."[1] Since he wrote these lines, twenty years ago, the number of Humanisms has increased significantly (although the number of French republics has remained stable). In recent years, for instance, the "secular humanists" have become objects of the scorn and contempt of the "Moral Majority." More traditionally, the word *Humanism* is used to describe the study of the Classics or, in a broader sense, the humanities. Yet with equal assurance it is employed to express respect for scientific knowledge. But since C. P. Snow has shown that these two cultures, the literary-artistic and the scientific-technological, are separated by a wide gulf, it is clear that the term *Humanism* has radically different connotations for these disciplines. The common denominator of all these definitions, if there is one, seems to be a concern with human values which are variously defined depending on the ideological stance of the user. It is obvious that such vague application of the term has reduced its usefulness considerably.

In this book, however, the term *Humanism* is used in its original and more precise sense to denote that literary and educational movement that started in the first third of the fourteenth century in Italy and spread all over Europe during the fifteenth and sixteenth centuries. Humanism was thus part of the Renaissance—an age of brilliant accomplishments in painting, architecture, music, sculpture, science, literature, and philosophy. This was a time when some of the most illustrious men of European cultural history lived: Leonardo da Vinci, Machiavelli, Albrecht Dürer, Hans Holbein,

Thomas More, Copernicus, Reuchlin, Erasmus, Luther, and Paracelsus, to mention only a few. It was also the age of great discoveries,
both geographical and intellectual. In 1492 Columbus discovered
a new continent which later came to be known as America. Fifty
years earlier Johannes Gutenberg had invented printing, thus making possible the fast dissemination of new ideas. In science Copernicus revolutionized our concept of the universe, and Martin Luther
shook the foundation of the Church with his Reformation.
Nevertheless, *Humanism* and *Renaissance* are not interchangeable
terms. Within the larger context of the Renaissance, which em-
braced all aspects of life, art, science, literature, architecture, and
politics, Humanism is a much narrower concept; and although "to
define the Renaissance in a sentence seems rather like rushing in
where not only angels but even fools would fear to tread,"[2] a widely
accepted definition of Humanism has emerged in recent years. According to this interpretation, Humanism was a movement that
stressed the study of "grammar, rhetoric, poetry, history and moral
philosophy" but excluded the study of natural philosophy, meta-
physics, and jurisprudence.[3] Central to the concerns of the humanists
were the *studia humanitatis*—a term which was first used in modern
times by Leonardo Bruni (1369–1444) at the beginning of the
fifteenth century. The term *humanitas* represents a conscious return
to the ancient word as it had been used fourteen hundred years
earlier by Varro, Cicero, and Aulus Gellius to designate "education
in the liberal arts" ("eruditio et institutio in bonas artes"). Already
Bruni had defined the goal of the *studia humanitatis:* they should
perfect and adorn man ("quod hominem perficiant atque exornent").
The claim that these disciplines were best suited for man's enno-
blement and the formation of a well-educated individual was not a
modest one, and it is understandable that Humanism, once it was
strong enough to be taken seriously, was bound to lead to clashes
with the established educational ideas with their stress on theology
and speculative philosophy.
    The *studia humanitatis* were taught by Humanists. The term *hu-
manista* or *umanista* as a label for the private and public teacher of
these studies first appeared in 1490 as a slang term coined by Italian
students in analogy to other terms for specialized teachers such as
legista or *jurista* for law professor or *alchemista* for the practitioner
of alchemy.[4] The word *Humanism* is of relatively recent origin. First
coined in German by the educator Franz Joseph Niethammer in

1808 to describe the emphasis placed on the Greek and Latin classics in secondary education as opposed to a more practice-oriented scientific training, it first appeared as a description for the literary movement in a book by Karl Hagen in 1841 but gained widespread popularity and acceptance only with Georg Voigt's classic book *Die Wiederbelebung des classischen Althertums oder das erste Jahrhundert des Humanismus* [The revival of classical antiquity or the first century of humanism, 1859]. From Germany the term spread to the other European countries.[5]

Since the decisive impulses for German Humanism came from Italy, a few words about Italian Humanism are in order. The key experience for the humanists was their encounter with classical antiquity which they claimed to have reawakened after a long sleep during the "dark" Middle Ages. Although this claim is certainly exaggerated, for the knowledge of the ancients had never really disappeared during that time, it is true that the attitude toward classical culture had changed significantly. While for the medieval writers pagan antiquity and the present flowed together, the Humanists realized the entirely different nature of the ancient Latin and Greek cultures. But in recognizing the different character of these past times they also adopted the classics as the norms and standards for their own writing and life-styles. Antiquity thus became a matter of a very personal world-view. Petrarch, for instance, wrote letters to ancient authors, such as Cicero, Seneca, and Livy, as if they were his personal friends. And the German Humanist Mutianus Rufus called antiquity a marriageable and beautiful virgin ("virgo nubilis et formosa"), saying "You are ravishingly beautiful, my love, and no blemishes are on you."[6]

It is, of course, not surprising that the revival of classical antiquity began in Italy. Here there were, after all, in the form of buildings or ruins, the witnesses, albeit mute, of Rome's former splendor. The consciousness that Rome had once been the center of a mighty empire had never completely disappeared. Roman history could be regarded as part of their own Italian past by the Humanists. Moreover, Italian was a language closely related to Latin.

With the discovery of the ancient world, the image of man also changed. During the Middle Ages man had been viewed as a member of a community or social group, such as a guild, a municipality, or a class. Now he was seen as a unique personality. This preoccupation with the individual is reflected in the literary genres pre-

ferred at the time. Biographies, letters, and accounts of personal
experiences became popular, just as in painting the portrait became
a favorite genre. Characteristic of this new emphasis on man is
Petrarch's experience in climbing Mont Ventoux in southern France
in 1336. Overpowered by the splendid view from the peak of that
mountain, he opened St. Augustine's *Confessions* at random. "Man,"
he read there, "admires the mountains, the sea, and the stars, but
he fails to admire himself." Struck by that passage, Petrarch realized
that nothing but the mind was admirable ("nihil praeter animum
esse mirabile") and decided to turn his eyes inwards ("in me ipsum
interiores oculos reflexi").[7] The German Humanist Rudolf Agricola
was only echoing his Italian colleagues when he said, "Prodigious,
immense, and unbelievable is the power of the human mind." A
little later Pico della Mirandola articulated these sentiments in his
famous speech *De dignitate hominis* [On the dignity of man, 1487],
a classic manifesto of Humanism: "Upon man, at the moment of
his creation, God bestowed seeds pregnant with all possibilities,
the germs of every form of life. Whichever of these a man shall
cultivate, the same will mature and bear fruit in him. . . . If
rational, he will reveal himself a heavenly being; if intellectual, he
will be an angel and the son of God."[8] While the Middle Ages had
seen man as a humble, fallen creature under the permanent curse
of original sin, Humanism believed in his dignity, power, and
greatness.

As a result of their admiration for the classical Latin authors, the
Humanists tried to write a purer, more elegant Latin than that
written during the Middle Ages by the Scholastics and the clergy.
Clarity and elegance of diction, modeled on Cicero's and Livy's prose,
henceforth became the ideals all Humanists strove for. This attention
to style explains the strong emphasis on language in the *studia
humanitatis,* covering both the grammatical-linguistic and the rhe-
torical-poetic aspects.

Petrarch's work was continued by others. Among those who had
significant influence on early German Humanism were Boccaccio,
Poggio, and Enea Silvio Piccolomini. At later stages of German
Humanism, Baptista Mantuanus, Marsilio Ficino, Guarino of Ve-
rona, and Pico della Mirandola exerted considerable influence also.
Their role will be discussed in the chapters concerned with those
German Humanists whom they inspired.

Chapter Two
Early Humanism
First Contacts in Prague

The first seeds of German Humanism were planted at the court of the German Emperor Charles IV (ruled 1346–1378) at Prague in the middle of the fourteenth century. By attracting artists and artisans, jurists and men of letters from all over Europe he had made this city the unequaled cultural center of the empire. During his reign, for instance, the famous cathedral of St. Vitus was built, the construction of the newer city was begun, and the first German university was founded.

In 1350 an Italian appeared in Prague, the first messenger of Humanism to the North. His name was Cola di Rienzo (1313–1354). He had seen the bitter political strife in Italy and especially in Rome where there continued to be constant fighting between the various powerful clans. Yet he was also keenly aware of the lost grandeur of Rome, having read Livy—or what was known of him at the time—and having deciphered with youthful enthusiasm the ancient Latin inscriptions. Thanks to his eminent rhetorical gifts he had been able to rouse the people to an insurrection against the noble families and, in a conscious attempt to revive ancient Roman institutions, had had himself elected tribune by the people. His reign, however, was short-lived, lasting less than seven months. In December, 1347, he was driven out of Rome by the fickle populace. Undaunted by this failure, he went to Prague, hoping to win Charles for his political plans. In a number of speeches delivered in elegant Latin before the court, the hot-blooded Italian tried to convince the emperor of the necessity of intervening in the Italian struggles and of working for a renewal *(renovatio)* of Italy's former greatness. Charles received his guest graciously, listening patiently to his orations and then—politely declining his request—had him jailed as a political liability. Evidently, Charles was a shrewd and cautious man who had been deeply disillusioned by his early experiences in Italian politics.

While Rienzo was still irritating his German hosts with ideas of a restitution of Rome's former glory and dazzling them with the elegance of his oratory, a letter arrived in 1351, written by none other than Francesco Petrarch, the most eminent man of letters in Europe at that time. In it the Italian Humanist also urged the monarch to use his prestige for the restitution of Rome's past splendor. Again, the realistic Charles remained deaf to the entreaties of his correspondent, but being a polite man he had to answer the letter. Unable to find anybody in his chancellery capable of composing an equally elegant response, he entrusted, of all men, Cola di Rienzo with the drafting of a polite but unequivocally negative reply. Subsequently Petrarch and Charles exchanged additional letters, and when Charles in 1354 crossed the Alps to receive the imperial crown, he and Petrarch met in Mantua. The coronation of the Emperor of the Holy Roman Empire of the German nation took place at Easter, 1355. Once again, Petrarch and his friends placed great expectations in the newly crowned emperor, hoping he would use his reputation to unite their tragically divided country. But before the sun had set on this day, the emperor and his small army turned their backs on Rome without having interfered in Italy's political struggle. With the disappearing army the dream of a political revival of Rome's glory was shattered. Henceforth this revival was limited to a restoration of the *studia humanitatis*. Instead of becoming a political force, Humanism was reduced to being a cultural and educational movement.[1]

One question that has often been asked is: what impact did these emissaries of Italian Humanism have on the North? The German scholar Konrad Burdach, for instance, saw in these contacts the beginnings of German Humanism. Here, he argued, a new prose style, a new eloquence, a new theory of letter-writing, and new literary genres developed. He considered *Der Ackermann aus Böhmen* [The plowman from Bohemia], which was written a generation later by Johann von Tepl, a direct fruit of this Bohemian early Humanism.[2] Serious doubts about this thesis were expressed, however, by Paul Joachimsen, who not only relativized Petrarch's and Rienzo's alleged influence on Prague, but also denied the connection between the culture that developed under Charles IV with that which we later call Humanism.[3] Most modern scholars seem to share the objections raised against the alleged transplantation of Italian Humanism to the North at this time. To be sure, although Charles and his court maintained a healthy skepticism toward the political visions of the two Italians, they were impressed by the rhetorical brilliance of Rienzo's speeches. Especially Johann von Neumarkt (1310–1380), the head of the imperial chancellery, became a great admirer of Petrarch and Rienzo. He had their letters copied and included partially as models in his *Summa Cancellaria,* a collection of model letters for his scribes. His own Latin clearly shows the influence of the new learning. It must also be granted that *Der Ackermann aus Böhmen* was affected by the novel rhetoric.

In historical perspective, however, the encounter with early Italian Humanism in Prague remained a short and isolated episode at the periphery of the empire, confined to a very small circle of men. The few tender seeds of Humanism that might have been planted were stamped out by the Hussite wars at the beginning of the fifteenth century. Modern scholars, therefore, tend to refer to this period not even as early Humanism but as Pre-Humanism or Proto-Humanism *(Vorhumanismus* or *Ersthumanismus).* Nevertheless, while these first contacts in the middle of the fourteenth century remained isolated instances, Humanist ideas began to be disseminated on a much wider scale during the next one hundred years. The reasons for this gradual diffusion of Humanism are multiple and complex. Here are but a few:

1. Attracted by the international prestige of transalpine schools of higher learning, hundreds of German students made their way across the Alps and enrolled in Italian universities. Although primarily journeying to Italy to study medicine or law, they often were exposed to Humanist teachers, thus acquiring a taste for the new learning. Very often they returned as enthusiastic devotees of the *studia humanitatis.* In fact, almost all German Humanists spent some time in Italy, and soon a pilgrimage to the Apennine peninsula became an absolute necessity.

2. In addition to such intellectual commerce, busy trade relations existed between southern Germany and Italy; these contributed in specific cases to the acceptance of Humanist ideas in Germany. Some German Humanists, such as Gossembrot in Augsburg and Pirckheimer in Nuremberg, were in fact wealthy merchants with literary interests.

3. Of great important to the spreading of Humanism was, of course, the invention of printing by Johannes Gutenberg in the middle of the fifteenth century. Quickly realizing the possibilities of that new art, the Humanists very often worked closely with the first printers.
4. While Italy certainly proved the decisive influence on the development of German Humanism, it can be argued that the soil had been prepared by local efforts. Foremost among those who can be claimed as precursors of Humanism are the members of the *Devotio Moderna,* or Brethren of the Common Life, who had encouraged the reading of the "safe" Classics.
5. The two great Church councils in the first half of the fifteenth century in Constance (1414–1418) and Basel (1431–1449) had brought to the North a great number of Italian Humanists. As ecclesiastical and diplomatic legates, as secretaries to princes and bishops, and as teachers of oratory and poetry, these rhetorically schooled Italians made a great impression on the German princes, who subsequently tried to secure their services. The Germans especially appreciated the elegant Latin cultivated by the Humanists, who could safely be entrusted with the composition of correspondence without causing their employers undue embarrassment. As envoys on diplomatic missions they could also hold their own in delivering brilliant and persuasive speeches.

Enea Silvio Piccolomini

One of the Italian Humanists who had made a deep impression on his northern friends at the Council of Basel and who later lived for many years in Germany was the Italian Enea Silvio Piccolomini (1405–1465), a man of letters, diplomat, churchman, and later Pope Pius II. Since he played a role in the transmission of Humanist ideas from Italy to Germany that earned him the title "apostle of Humanism to Germany" by his great biographer Georg Voigt, he will be discussed here in some detail.[4]

Born of a noble but poor family, Piccolomini spent his years of study in Siena and Florence. At the age of twenty-six he attended the Council of Basel as secretary to several bishops and one cardinal. In 1443 Emperor Frederick III appointed him secretary to the imperial chancellery, which had been moved from Prague to Vienna only three years before. During his many years in Basel and Vienna Enea kept up an untiring propaganda campaign for Humanism, stressing in innumerable letters, speeches, and treatises the value of the *studia humanitatis*.

It would be wrong to assume, however, that the emperor had engaged Enea out of love for Humanism. Frederick was a thrifty and sober man with no deep understanding for the new learning. His main reason for bringing the Italian to Vienna had been Enea's reputation as a brilliant Latin orator and stylist. Although his reception at the court and at the university was cool, he was enthusiastically received by his colleagues in the chancellery. To be sure, no famous names are among those who, influenced by his ideas, spread the Humanist gospel once they left Vienna and assumed positions elsewhere. But the history of German Humanism is not only the chronicle of well-known names but also the story of scores of lesser-known men who worked quietly and patiently in small cities and sometimes at tiny secular or ecclesiastical courts. They are individuals often known only to local historians but without whose work Humanism would not have had the impact it had in the sixteenth century.

One figure—not a member of the chancellery—may be singled out as having been decisively influenced by Piccolomini; that man was Niclas von Wyle, the first and perhaps the most important of the early German Humanists (see p. 16), who became one of Enea's most fervent popularizers. Of his eighteen translations, published in 1478, four were renderings of works by the Italian, among them the long and excellent translation of Enea's timeless and compelling novella *Eurialus and Lucretia*. Wyle was also the first to edit the collected letters of the Italian Humanist, thus making them available to the educated German public as models of the new epistolary art cultivated in Italy.

Although Enea's impact extended to various fields, it was deepest and most enduring in historiography, and among the numerous historical works it was his *Germania* or *Teutonia* that had the greatest influence.[5] It was written in response to a complaint by the German clergyman Martin Mayer, chancellor to the archbishop of Mainz, who, in congratulating Enea on his elevation to the cardinalship, used the occasion to remind him of the many grievances the German nation had against the Roman Curia. Rome, argued Mayer, seems bent on sapping the German nation of its strength and substance. Through the heavy burdens placed upon it, the "once proud nation of the Germans has been reduced to beggary, subjected to humil-

iating exactions, and left to cower in the dust bemoaning its misery."
If nothing is done, the chancellor threatens, the princes will rise
against the Curia.[6]

Enea's reply, usually entitled *De ritu, situ, moribus et conditione
Germaniae* [On the customs, location, manners, and condition of
Germany, 1457] or simply *Germania* is divided into three books.
In the first book Enea attempts to refute specific charges, saying
that the grievances catalogued by Mayer either did not exist or were
trivial. In the third book the Italian Humanist declares that rebellion
would be folly, asking for the names of those princes who would
dare to oppose Rome. A long list of the German ecclesiastical princes
and their alleged loyalties follows. However, for the cultural and
literary historian it is the second book that holds special interest
and fascination, for it contains a detailed description of the cultural
and geographical physiognomy of fifteenth-century Germany. But
before Enea paints this portrait of contemporary Germany, he describes in graphic detail the ancient, primitive Germanic times:

Little differed your ancestors' life at that time from that of wild animals:
for the most part they were shepherds living in forests and woodlands
. . . They had neither fortified cities nor towns surrounded by walls; no
castles perched high on mountains, no temples built out of hewn stone
were to be seen. Absent were the pleasures of gardens and country houses,
no parks, no plantations, no valleys like the one in ancient Tempe, were
cultivated. . . They had little silver, less gold; the use of pearls was
unknown, no ostentatious display of jewels, no purple and silken dresses
. . . Writing was unknown, there was no jurisprudence; liberal arts and
the sciences were not studied. Religion itself was barbarous, absurd idol-
atry. Indeed it was so corrupted through the delusion of demons that often
human sacrifices were made. Gang robberies were praised; everything was
horrible, shocking, gross, and brutal.[7]

This picture of Germany's barbarous past is then contrasted with
her thriving and prosperous present:

. . . everywhere we see cultivated fields, flourishing crops, vineyards,
gardens, flower beds, orchards in the country and in the suburbs, buildings
filled with precious objects, charming country-houses, castles high on
mountains, towns surrounded by walls, and splendid cities.[8]

And then Enea portrays more than twenty of these splendid German
cities in detail and many more in passing, describing the flourishing

universities, pointing to the many high-yielding gold and silver mines, and giving a vivid account of the magnificent secular and ecclesiastical architecture.

There was, of course, method in this flattery. For if Mayer had contended that once rich and mighty Germany had been reduced to poverty, Enea claimed that the opposite was in fact the case and that this miraculous transformation was solely due to the Christianization by Rome. Heavy taxes, he suggested, were the price the Germans had to pay for having been changed by the Roman Church from a barbaric and poor province into a civilized and prosperous country.

Written in polished Latin and with an astonishingly detailed knowledge of his host country, this treatise had an enormous influence on future German Humanists, which, however, came to be felt only after it had appeared in print in 1496. This impact can be seen in three areas.

First, following Enea, German historians increasingly turned away from the old fables of the German past with their stories about the Trojan origins of the ancient Germans, relying instead more on Roman and Greek historians, such as Caesar, Tacitus, and Strabo. Criticism of these sources, however clumsily and hesitantly done, thus replaced the former dependence on the stories and unbridled fantasies of previous chroniclers.

Second, Enea's *Germania* supplied later historians with a wealth of motifs, themes, and topics. It introduced, for instance, the motif of the reappearance of the ancient German hero who is so puzzled by the many positive changes that he can hardly recognize his own country. Furthermore, the Italian Enea did not hesitate to rate the Germans militarily superior to his own countrymen, citing as proof the defeat the Roman general Quintilius Varus suffered at the hands of the Germans in A.D. 9. The *cladis Variana,* the defeat of Varus, was to become an important commonplace with later Humanists. Enea also took the territorial princes to task, chiding them for letting the empire fall from its height and pleading with them to set aside divisiveness, disobedience, and egotism. Finally, the comparison between the old and modern Germany set an important precedent for future historians.

Third, Enea not only provided the German Humanists with certain phrases, key motifs, and important ideas, he also acquainted them with an author who soon was to become their favorite Latin

historian: the Roman Cornelius Tacitus (ca. A.D. 55–116/120). The
latter's description of Germany, also called *Germania,* had a decisive
influence on their thinking. This work, together with two minor
works, the *Dialogus* and *De Agricola* [About Agricola], had been
discovered only a few decades prior to Enea's *Germania.* To be sure,
Enea freely manipulated Tacitus in his tendentious selection of facts.
For instance, in order to show the great debt the Germans owed to
Rome he intentionally emphasized particularly primitive features in
ancient Germany, contrasting them with the wealth and prosperity
of the present day. But his merit lies in making the Germans aware
of the existence of Tacitus. And when they studied the Roman
historian themselves they read him with different eyes than Enea
had done. Although Tacitus had depicted the ancient Germans as
primitive and barbarous, he also had praised them for their honesty,
bravery, hospitality, and integrity, even setting them up as models
for his spoilt, degenerate, and corrupt contemporaries, the Romans
of the first century A.D. Here the Humanists found a Germany they
did not have to be ashamed of.

The importance of Tacitus to the Humanists was not only that
he painted a positive picture of ancient Germany but also that he
looked at it as a unity—an idea that probably would have surprised
the various Germanic tribes of that time. Fourteen hundred years
later it took again the objectivity of a foreigner to break down the
narrow confines of regionalism and tribal patriotism and to point
out the common elements of the German lands. For up to that time
the Germans had seen themselves either as citizens of a European
Christian community or as inhabitants of certain regions, such as
Bavaria, Saxony, or Franconia. Enea made them aware of their cultural uniqueness and common achievements. He thus contributed
substantially to the development of a German national consciousness. It is, of course, not without irony that a non-German, a citizen
of a country that at that time looked down on the Germans as
barbarians, unwittingly became the father of German nationalism.

Peter Luder (ca. 1415–1472)

Only hesitantly did the German universities open their doors to
Humanism. Among those who spread this new educational program
at these institutions of higher learning, the so-called wandering
Humanists played a prominent role. Since the study of the Classics

was not part of the university curriculum at that time, the teachers of these studies depended not only on the goodwill of their more traditional colleagues but also on the lecture fees of their own students. Under these circumstances, the wandering of scholars from one university to the next was not so much an expression of a restless spirit as an economic necessity.

Fairly typical of that small but intrepid group of traveling Humanists who tried to secure a niche for classical studies at the German universities was Peter Luder. The following distich succinctly sums up Luder's perception of himself: claiming to have been the first to have brought to Germany the muses, the recognition that poetry, as he understood it, was Italian in origin, and the acknowledgment that Guarino of Ferrara was his teacher and inspiration:

> Primus ego in patriam deduxi vertice Musas
> Italico mecum, fonte Guarino tuo.
> (I was the first who led from Italian summits
> home to my country the muse, Guarino being my source.)[9]

Born around 1415, Luder enrolled at the age of fifteen at the University of Heidelberg. Without finishing his bachelor of arts degree he left that city and went to Italy sometime before 1434. After traversing Italy and possibly Greece, he began to study medicine at the University of Ferrara. Like many of his fellow students from the North, however, he was more attracted by the lectures on classical authors than by medical discourses. In Ferrara the famous Guarino introduced him to the *studia humanitatis*. Henceforth Luder considered it his task to campaign for them just as forcefully as Piccolomini had done a decade earlier. After nearly twenty years in the South he returned to Germany in 1456. With the moral but hardly financial support of Elector Frederick of the Palatinate he began to give lectures at his old alma mater, the University of Heidelberg. His inaugural lecture, delivered on July 15, 1456, is an important document of early German Humanism.[10] After a brief autobiographical sketch and some remarks on the traditional university subjects, Luder devotes himself to the *studia humanitatis,* a term which he introduced to Germany and by which he primarily meant rhetoric, poetry, and history. Although he met with some resistance from scholastically oriented professors, it has been shown that there was no widespread animosity toward the new studies. As a matter of fact, Luder counted among his friends and acquaintances prominent members of the theological faculty, such as Johannes Wenck, Jodocus Eichmann, and Johannes Ernesti.

Subsequently Luder lectured on Valerius Maximus, Horace, Seneca, Terence, and Ovid. During this time he also composed a lengthy love poem, the *Elegia ad Panphilam* [Elegy to Panphila],[11] in which he expressed in very explicit terms his love for the girl Panphila. He later declared that this poem was meant as an allegory, symbolizing his devotion to his patron, the Elector. Whether Luder, who was not without a mischievous sense of humor, was serious about this matter or whether he said this tongue-in-cheek to curry favor with Frederick in the hope of receiving increased financial support is a moot question. If the latter was his intention, it failed, for he had to leave Heidelberg in 1460. It is not quite clear why. Possibly his unorthodox life-style, complete with amatory adventures and carousing in the Heidelberg student pubs, offended his stuffy colleagues; possibly it was the economic necessity of finding new students elsewhere that prompted him to depart. In the next few years Luder made brief guest appearances in Ulm and at the universities of Erfurt and Leipzig. At all three places he was received warmly. In Leipzig, where a small circle of young men interested in Humanistic studies had already gathered, he promised in the public announcement of his lectures not only to enlighten his students on Virgil, Terence, and Latin metrics but also to teach them purer and more stylish Latin. In this notice, however, he committed the unpardonable sin of using an accusative instead of dative with the verb *interesse*. His opponents were, of course, quick to point out that embarrassing error.[12]

Luder returned to Padua in the fall of 1462 to take up his long-neglected medical studies, becoming a doctor in 1464. In the same year he was engaged by the newly founded University of Basel. The thrifty burghers (in contrast to most other German universities the University of Basel was founded and financed by the city and not by a sovereign) employed him in a triple function: as a *poeta* or Humanist he had to give lectures on Latin poetry, as a physician he was a member of the medical school, and as a city doctor he had to take care of the sick. Toward the end of his life he was briefly employed by Duke Sigismund of Tyrolia as a speaker and diplomat on several missions. He died in 1472.

Luder's literary oeuvre is a modest one consisting of his inaugural lecture, a few poems, a number of speeches, and some rather frank letters to his friend Mathias von Kemnat which have earned him the reputation of a man about town. His inaugural lecture of 1456 on the value of the *studia humanitatis* was a mosaic of notes from lectures by his Ferrara teacher, Guarino. Although it was largely derivative, Luder was proud enough of it to present it, in slightly modified form, successively at the universities of Heidelberg, Erfurt, Basel, and probably Vienna. His two longer poems, *Elegia ad Panphilam* and *Ad Mavortium virum Fridericum* [To the martial man Frederick][13] are modeled on the classical Roman elegy, full of allusions to Latin literature and ancient mythology. One looks, of course, in vain for any originality or expression of personal feeling in them—a criticism that could also be leveled against much of the poetry written by the later German Humanists. But not originality but unabashed imitation and emulation were their goal. Luder not only imitated the form but also took up many of the themes of Latin poetry. He maintained, for instance, that only the poet is able to immortalize his subject. Solely through his verses will Panphila acquire eternal fame:

> Forma bonum fragile est, nec quicquam corporis adest
>   stare diu poterit, vates habendus erit,
> Qui tua gesta canat tollatque ad sidera caeli
>   Te, nam digna dea es, ac superis similis.

> (Physical beauty is fleeting, all of your body will vanish,
>   Everything withers away; unless the poet appears,
> singing your deeds in high praise and lifting you up to the skies,
>   worthy to be labeled divine, bearing resemblance to gods.)[14]

Regrettably, Luder made very sparing use of his gift for immortalizing other people through poetry. Yet it would be wrong to judge him by his small literary output. Equally important is the personal influence he exerted on an astonishing number of young men, among them Hartmann Schedel, the author of the *Nuremberg Chronicle* (1493). The modern scholar Frank Baron, who has traced Luder's influence in painstaking research, has arrived at the following conclusion: "The historian of early humanism today can easily find traces of Luder at all the major universities of this time. Luder's influence emerges as a significant factor in the shaping of the intellectual changes of this era."[15]

And indeed these intellectual changes were slowly but inevitably taking place. Luder was followed by other wandering Humanists like Samuel Karoch von Lichtenberg,[16] the Italian Petrus Antonius Finarensis, and the Spaniard Jacobus Publicius. In the 1480s and 1490s more permanent positions for classical studies were established, although the Humanist lectures amounted only to a very small portion of the total curricular offerings. Humanism was still leading a very quiet and unassuming existence. This changed only with the emergence of more aggressive figures like Jakob Locher and Conrad Celtis toward the end of the century.

Early Humanist Translators

While the personal influence of Peter Luder and the other wandering Humanists was considerable, their literary works, all in Latin, were unimpressive. More important, both in quality and in quantity, was the work done in German by the early Humanist translators. Without question it is in the area of translation, which includes adaptations and other transformations, that these representatives of the first phase of German Humanism excelled. It can therefore safely be said that early German Humanism produced primarily a literature of translations.

In assessing the value of these translations we should not forget that literary historians have not always done justice to the art of translating, often regarding its practitioners as lacking creativity and even showing literary impotence. Such critics completely ignore the fact that most great literature is the result of a dialectical interplay of outside inspiration and personal creativity. Reception of foreign influences is therefore an indispensable prerequisite for the creation of an indigenous literature.

Niclas von Wyle.   In 1452 Niclas von Wyle wrote a letter to Enea Silvio Piccolomini which was answered in the most flattering terms by the Italian Humanist. Praising his correspondent for his rhetorical and artistic talents—Wyle had sent along one of his paintings—Enea expressed the hope that the German would bring eloquence to a new flowering in his native land. In the following two and a half decades the German Humanist tried to fulfill the hopes Enea had placed in him, though possibly in quite a different way than the Italian had expected. Wyle became the first and perhaps the most important translator of Italian and Latin literature of that generation.

Born in Bremgarten, Switzerland, in 1410, Niclas von Wyle spent more than twenty years as town clerk *(Stadtschreiber)* in the Swabian city of Esslingen and the last eight years of his life as second chancellor of Count Ulrich of Württemberg. Held in high esteem because of his tact and diplomatic skill and extremely well connected with members of the nobility, he was occasionally engaged by other cities and princes for special diplomatic missions. Among his many acquaintances he counted Countess Palatine Mechthild (1418–1482), the co-founder of the universities of Freiburg (1457) and Tübingen (1477). She was a just and competent ruler who had made her court in Rottenburg on the Neckar the center of intellectual and literary activities in southern Germany. Wyle was the dominating figure at this court.

During his years in Esslingen Wyle directed a private school, instructing young men of noble families in the art of writing, poetics, stylistics, and orthography. Initially translating Latin texts into German only for his students, as his fame spread he was asked by several princes and princesses to translate some of these Latin pieces for them. Beginning in 1461 individual translations were periodically printed. Shortly before his death in 1478 he published the entire sequence of eighteen in Esslingen with the printing house of Konrad Fyner. They became known under the title *Translatzion oder Tütschungen* [Translations or Germanizations].[17]

Throughout these works Wyle comments in such detail on the art of translation that there is no doubt that his efforts were the product of long and careful deliberation. As a result, he can be called the first German Humanist who systematically reflected on the rules, tasks, and problems of translation.

Following a suggestion from Gregor Heimburg, the well-known lawyer and statesman from Nuremberg, that any elegant Latin text, properly translated, would inevitably produce stylish German,[18] Wyle produced translations that were as literal as he could make them. The recognized superiority of Latin was intended to be transferred to the German despite that language's clumsiness and inadequacy. In the desire to discipline German by subjecting it to the structure and grammar of Latin, the Swabian Humanist did not hesitate to graft Latin constructions upon the vernacular, using, for example, the unusual if not impossible accusative with infinitive and participial constructions, regardless of the entirely different character of German and of the effect upon readability. Thus he translated the Latin sentence "Sed invenies aliquos senes amantes, amatum nullum" with "du findest aber etlich alt liebhabend mane, aber liebgehapten kainen" instead of saying, as he himself suggests, "du findest aber etlich alt mane die frowen liebhapent. Aber kainen alten findest du, der von frowen wird lieb gehapt" ("but you will find some old loving men but none loved" instead of "but you will find some old men who love women but no old one who is loved by women").[19]

It is this wrestling with an undeveloped language, this slavish imitation of Latin that has provoked alternately praise and condemnation by critics. The controversy surrounding his translation methods has almost obscured the fact that Wyle occupies a key position in the introduction of fresh and modern subject matter to German culture, and that he was, in fact, a pioneer who belonged to what we now might call the avant-garde writers of the day. Even a cursory glance at the authors he translated will confirm this impression. First of all, it is surprising that at a time that is characterized by the slogan of the renewal of antiquity none of the authors translated is Greek or Roman, with the exception of Lucian whose *Golden Ass,* however, Wyle characteristically translated from Poggio's Latin version. And it is Poggio, the author of the witty and bawdy *Facetiae* [Humorous pieces], who, with six pieces, leads the authors translated, followed by Enea Silvio, who is represented with four works. Petrarch, Boccaccio, and Leonardo Bruni appear with one selection each. In other words, the authors Wyle was interested in were either the progressive writers of the day or somewhat older ones representing early Italian Humanism. In any case, they were the representatives of a new Humanistic spirit and a new image of man.

In order to give his readers an idea of the scope of this new Humanistic writing, Wyle included in his anthology a great variety of literary genres, ranging from personal letters, witty conversations and table talks, dialogues, a skillfully built oration, treatises, and a novel to the gems of the Italian novella. This diversity of genres is matched by the variety of topics: the power of love, hospitality, the feasibility of marriage for elderly men, the prudent management of a household, the character of mendicant friars, the vicissitudes of fortune, the value of Humanist studies, true nobility versus nobility of birth, praise of women, friendship, and the necessity of correct spelling.

Wyle's masterpiece is, without doubt, his rendering of Enea's novella *De Eurialo et Lucretia* [Eurialus and Lucretia]. What is new in this love story about a handsome German knight in the retinue of Emperor Sigismund and a married lady in Siena is the astonishing realism, outspoken sensuality, and psychological insight. Love is depicted as an almost divine force engulfing reason and respectability. Both in the Latin original (1444) and Wyle's lively translation (1462)—the first into any vernacular—it became a bestseller. Its success must seem somewhat surprising at a time when the public was used to action-packed novels with adventures of knights endlessly strung together. This story, on the other hand, by virtue of its strict structure, its minimal action, and its emphasis on the depiction of emotions rather than on suspense-filled episodes, was bound eventually to change the taste of the reading public.

Love is also the theme of the second *Translatze,* the novella *Guiscard and Sigismunda* from Boccaccio's *Decameron,* which Wyle translated from Leonardo Bruni's Latin version. It is the story of a love affair between a girl and a young man of noble heart but low birth. The lovers are caught by her father; Guiscard is killed and his heart is brought to Sigismunda on a silver platter. More interesting than the gory ending is the ensuing confrontation between father and daughter. The father's reproach, for instance, that she should at least have selected a lover of noble descent is unmasked as a hypocritical double standard: "But that I am criticized for his low birth. In this you are following the illusion of the mob and common people and you fail to see that you do not criticize Guiscard but fortune which generally elevates those who are unworthy and suppresses those who are worthy."[20] Moreover, the right of a woman to take the initiative in such an affair is energetically defended. A new concept of the female sex emerges, worlds apart from that of the Middle Ages and that found in the popular literature of the time.

On an entirely different level but equally modern and daring was the choice of the subject matter of Wyle's eleventh translation. It is Poggio's letter to his friend Leonardo Aretino about the burning of Jerome of Prague during the Council of Constance. Though Poggio stresses his belief in the wisdom of the Council's decision, he hardly conceals his admiration for the Bohemian heretic. Quoting in detail the magnificent speech Jerome made in his defense before

he was burnt, the Italian sees in him not only an excellent representative of the new eloquence but also praises him for his courage.
This letter is fairly typical of the conflict arising between the Humanists and the overwhelming authority of the Church.

Again in a different area but just as bold was Wyle's translation
of Enea's letter to Duke Sigismund of Tyrolia, the tenth *Translatze*.
In this famous plea for the *studia humanitatis,* which toward the end
is expanded into a *Fürstenspiegel* [Mirror for princes], Enea—and,
of course, tacitly Wyle—voices sentiments that are considerably
ahead of his time. Enea's statement, for instance, that a state should
not exist for its sovereign but that the sovereign should be the first
servant of the state, clearly anticipates ideas expressed in the eighteenth century. Moreover, at a time when entire books were written
about the correct form of address, Enea's defense of the familiar *Du,*
as opposed to the formally acceptable *Sie,* was likely to raise the
eyebrows of his blue-blooded recipient, in Wyle's case Charles of
Baden.

Despite these works, however, Enea's hope that Wyle would bring
eloquence to a flowering in Germany was not fulfilled at the time.
Wyle's attempts to reform the German language must be dismissed
as well-intentioned but essentially misguided efforts. His primary
significance lies in the transmission of new literary subject matter.
Sensing what was new and modern in Petrarch, Poggio, Boccaccio,
and Silvio Piccolomini, the Swabian Humanist made them accessible
to his countrymen through his translations. With that he contributed substantially to the widening of the literary horizons and re-
fining of the tastes of the German reading public of the second half
of the fifteenth century.

Albrecht von Eyb.   Albrecht von Eyb, the second important
exponent of early German Humanism, was born in 1420, a scion
of an old Franconian baronial family. After attending the *Lateinschule*
in Rotenburg ob der Tauber and briefly the University of Erfurt,
he went, like so many other northern Humanists, to Italy. During
two extended stays, interrupted by one year in Germany, he studied
law at the universities of Pavia, Bologna, and Padua, completing
his studies and becoming a doctor of canon and Roman law. Altogether he spent almost one and a half decades on the Apennine
peninsula. In 1449 he became canon in Bamberg and ten years later
also in Eichstätt. Because of his legal training he was often consulted
by cities and princes. He died in 1475.

Eyb returned from his first stay in Italy (1444–1451) without an academic degree but with considerable enthusiasm for the *studia humanitatis*. This enthusiasm found expression in a number of Latin works which might be called the first Humanist writings by a German, predating Peter Luder's earliest literary attempts by half a decade. Among them is a rather frivolous work on the alleged moral corruption of the women of Bamberg, a city to which he had returned to satisfy the residency requirements as a canon. Entirely different in tone from this *Appellatio mulierum Bambergensium* [Appeal of the women of Bamberg] is his *Ad laudem et commendationem Bambergae civitatis* [Speech in praise and commendation of the community of Bamberg].[21] Modeled on a praise of Pavia by his teacher Balthasar Rasinus and possibly influenced by the brilliant sketches of towns Enea Silvio had interspersed in his letters and historical writings, this work describes in its first part the natural amenities and surroundings of this picturesque city. The second part offers a survey of Bamberg's magnificent secular and sacral buildings, her political institutions and inhabitants, while dwelling in particular on the piety of the clergy, the *humanitas* of its citizens, and the integrity and respectability of its women. If the latter commendation seems surprising in light of the flippant treatment of Bamberg's fair sex in the *Appellatio,* it has to be remembered that each work was addressed to a different audience: the first, the *Appellatio,* was intended for his ecclesiastical colleagues on the hill, which, with its churches, episcopal residence, and houses for the canons, was almost a city in itself, while the second was meant for the townspeople in the valley.

Also intended for his fellow canons in Bamberg, but again in an entirely different vein was Eyb's eulogy of the Holy Eucharist called *Laudatio de divinissimo eucharisticae sacramento* [Praise of the most divine sacrament of the Eucharist]. It was delivered as a sermon on Maundy Thursday, 1452. Richly interlaced with Latin hexameters and references to ancient mythology—Ceres and Bacchus are described, for instance, as metaphorical representations of bread and wine—it must have sounded rather strange to his colleagues, who were still untouched by this typically Humanist synthesis of pagan and Christian elements.

Eyb's voluminous *Margarita poetica* [Poetic pearl, completed in 1459, printed 1472] is essentially an anthology of Latin works, consisting of excerpts from Roman, patristic, and Humanist literature, both in prose and verse, as well as extracts from Latin dramatic literature. In addition thirty speeches are included, among them Eyb's sermon on the Eucharist and his praise of Bamberg. At a time when only very few manuscript editions of the classical authors were available, Eyb in *Margarita* gave his contemporaries a book in which he had collected the best, or what he considered the best, of the Latin literature of the three different periods. Therein clearly lies its cultural-historical significance. That there was a real need for this kind of work is attested by the frequency of the reprints. Between 1472 and 1503 no fewer than fifteen different editions appeared in Germany, France, and Italy. For thirty years the *Margarita* became something like the bible of German Humanism. Only when the works of the ancient authors became available in complete editions did the demand for this book abate.

In the discharge of his various administrative, ecclesiastical, and legal duties, Eyb had ample opportunity to reflect on the social institution of marriage. It is no wonder, then, that his preoccupation with this topic found expression not only in some shorter works but also in his long treatise on the question of whether a man should take a wife or not, generally referred to as the *Ehebüchlein* [Book on marriage].

Dedicated to the council and citizens of Nuremberg "for strengthening their government and public authorities," the book is divided into three parts of varying length. In the first part the reasons against marriage are enumerated and themes like chastity, female beauty, fertility, children's education, dowry, and the turmoil of conjugal battles are discussed. The second part, conceived as an antithesis to the first, answers the question initially posed with a clear and unequivocal yes, ending with a short but impressive praise of matrimony. To illustrate the points that "women and virgins should be given husbands in time" and "how a woman should behave during the absence of her husband" two novellas, *Guiscard and Sigismunda* and *Marina,* are inserted. The third part is concerned with table manners at weddings and the "misery," disease, and repulsiveness of human nature." To exemplify the notion that "no sinner should abandon hope" Eyb tells the gruesome legend of *Albanus* who, born in incest, out of revenge kills his father and mother, who is, of course, at the same time his wife and his sister. After an inner conversion he finds his way back to the repentent life of a saint.

The *Ehebüchlein* offers a refreshingly new attitude toward both women and marriage. Neither lapsing into the misogynic pose found in much of the popular literature of the time, nor indulging in an ahistorical glorification of the female sex, Eyb paints a realistic picture of women, at the same time taking those to task who treat women unfairly. In doing this, he occasionally sounds like a twentieth-century feminist, as when he criticizes the sexual double standards: "How is it possible," he asks, for instance, "that the husband demands chastity from his wife without observing it himself? How is it possible that men excuse themselves with nice words while condemning and punishing their wives?" Or: "If a husband commits adultery and the wife learns about it, this is considered fun and amusement and is not punished. But if the wife just leaves the house, she has done wrong and is punished." In a society that treats both sexes so unequally the bleak situation of a woman can be summed up only in this way: "Women have a difficult law and a hard life and they are in a much worse situation than men." Hand in hand with this realistic appraisal of the situation of women goes a renewed emphasis on the joys of matrimonial life: ". . . marriage is a merry, sensuous, and sweet thing. What can be more joyous and sweeter than the name of the father, the mother and the children hanging around the necks of their parents and receiving many a sweet kiss from them?"[22]

If the *Ehebüchlein* is thoroughly imbued with the spirit of Humanism, the *Spiegel der Sitten* [Mirror of manners, written 1474, printed posthumously in 1511] is based primarily on medieval and patristic sources. This "regression," if indeed it can be called that, points to the transitional character of the age when Humanist and medieval tendencies could occasionally be discerned in the very same author. Whether Eyb turned to medieval topics to ingratiate himself with his more conservative ecclesiastical colleagues who rightly suspected him of Humanist leanings, or whether this new interest in the Middle Ages was a reflection of his true nature, is unclear. In any case, this criticism can only be leveled against the first part of the book in which he discusses death, the seven deadly sins, and the various social classes.

The second part offers German translations of two comedies by Plautus, the *Menaechmi* and the *Bacchides,* as well as the translation of the *Philogenia* by the Italian Humanist Ugolino de Pisanis. It is these translations that have elicited the undivided applause of the critics. Unlike Wyle, Eyb believed that an original should not be translated word by word but according to the sense. Eyb's goal was, therefore, not a translation of ancient drama, but its transplantation into the world of the German fifteenth century. In order to achieve this goal he substituted, for instance, names like Götz, Fritz, Lutz, and Barb—familiar to his German audience through the *Fastnachtsspiele* [Shrovetide plays]—for foreign-sounding Latin and Greek ones. References to Roman institutions and offices also fell victim to his attempts to transform the comedies of Plautus into fifteenth-century German plays. They are either completely dropped or boldly germanized. The same fate befalls mythological allusions which are eliminated or Christianized. Numerous additions in which Eyb tries to surpass the original with coarse humor also makes the text more lively. The choice of translating these comedies into prose and not the somewhat awkward doggerel popular at the time also contributed to this liveliness. Eyb was not only the first but for a long time also the best translator of Plautus. We have to wait until the eighteenth century when J. M. R. Lenz wrote his *Lustspiele nach dem Plautus* [Comedies after Plautus] to see the comedies of the Roman poet rendered into German with similar skill and freshness. For that reason alone Eyb deserves an important place in the history of German literature.

Heinrich Steinhöwel. Heinrich Steinhöwel was almost fifty years old when he began his literary career. Born in Weil near Stuttgart in 1412, he attended the University of Vienna where he obtained the bachelor's and master's degrees; in 1438 he went to Padua, which had the reputation of having the best and most progressive medical school in Italy. Returning in 1443 as doctor of medicine, he was briefly associated with the University of Heidelberg and then, in 1450, accepted the appointment of city physician of Ulm for the sizable annual salary of one hundred guilders plus six days' paid vacation. He held this position until his death in 1478.

Like Wyle, he concentrated almost exclusively on translations, saying jokingly in the preface of his *Apollonius of Tyre:*

> Eigen gedicht wer mer ze schwer,
> Latin ze tütschen ist min ger.

(Writing my own poems is too hard.
Translating Latin to German is what I like.)

And this is precisely what he did and excelled in, the choice of his translation being determined by his years in Italy and his exposure to the *studia humanitatis*. Of the more than seven major works he translated, at least four deserve brief mention.

Griseldis (1461/62) is the story of a poor and beautiful peasant girl who is married by the margrave, dutifully bears him two children, but then is subjected to a series of extremely cruel obedience trials by her husband which she endures—and passes—with admirable patience. The margrave, having thus assured himself of her constancy and virtuousness, reveals his true and allegedly well-meaning intentions and the couple lives happily ever after. Boccaccio was the first to make use of the old fairy-tale motif in a literary form, employing it in the one hundredth story of his *Decameron*. In that work he told the story in thoroughly human terms: while Griseldis is portrayed with considerable sympathy, the margrave is described as a despicable man, a characterization most modern readers probably would share. But it was not Boccaccio's Italian version but Petrarch's Latin adaptation that made the story widely known in Europe. Petrarch, however, gave it an entirely new emphasis, portraying the margrave in a much more positive light. Thus the story became a paradigm of a wife's blind obedience to her husband and, by extension, man's blind trust in God. It was this version that Steinhöwel translated into German. The preference given to Petrarch's moralizing version over Boccaccio's is a reflection of Steinhöwel's taste. Like Eyb, he was both a Humanist and a pious moralist.

In 1473 Steinhöwel's translation of Boccaccio's *De claris mulieribus* [On famous women] appeared under the title *Von den synnrychen erluchten wyben* [On wise and illustrious women]. The ninety-nine biographies of famous women, ranging from Greek mythology to contemporary history, are preceded by a preface addressed to Archduchess Eleonore of Austria, the daughter of King James I of Scotland and since 1449 wife of Duke Sigismund of Tyrolia. As the translator of the French knightly novel *Pontus and Sidonia*, Eleonore, who had made the Innsbruck court a center for artists, had herself pioneered the prose novel in Germany. In his preface Steinhöwel apologizes for having to include the biographies of immoral women,

justifying such inclusions with the argument that they might serve
as deterrents, while their virtuous counterparts are to be regarded
as shining examples. That Eleonore is considered by Steinhöwel a
pinnacle of virtuous women should come as no surprise, and he
promises to devote the one hundredth chapter to her as the crowning
representative of all women. Either he forgot this promise in course
of time or he had meant it only symbolically in any case: the one
hundredth chapter is devoted, quite prosaically, to the rules of
punctuation.

Like Eyb, Steinhöwel placed the emphasis on the rendering of
sense rather than individual words, allowing himself considerable
freedom with the text, abridging some stories, leaving out others
and even adding several of his own. Occasionally he felt obliged to
disassociate himself from some of the more risqué stories, claiming
that it is not "proper for us Christians to write that."[23] At one point
he softens Boccaccio's harsh criticism of the degenerate nobility,
saying that the abuses happened not here but "beyond the sea."[24]
He must have forgotten that Eleonore had come from precisely
"beyond the sea."

Illustrated with splendid woodcuts, *Von den synnrychen erluchten
wyben* was received well, both by the general public and by Eleonore
herself. Out of gratitude for this friendly reception, Steinhöwel
dedicated his next undertaking to her husband, Duke Sigismund
of Tyrolia. This translation is that of the *Speculum vitae humanae*
[The mirror of human life] by the Spanish theologian, jurist, and
diplomat Rodriguez Sanchez de Arevala (1404–1470). In the first
of the two parts the social classes, "from the emperor to the shepherd,"
pass in review with their positive and negative sides, while in the
second part he critically portrays the different ranks of the ecclesiastical
hierarchy, "from the pope to the sexton." Because Rodriguez
spared neither the clergy nor the Roman Curia in his criticism, the
Lutherans later claimed him as a precursor of their faith—a claim
that can be justified only with difficulty since criticism of the Church
was so widespread at the time that virtually every critic would have
to be called a Proto-Lutheran.

As in his other works, Steinhöwel tried to convey the general
meaning rather than give a literal translation. The result is concrete
and lively prose which does full justice to the German language.
Following his popularizing intentions, Steinhöwel, on the one hand,
shortens or eliminates the numerous philosophical digressions of the

original, adding, on the other, colorful descriptions of fifteenth-century life. In doing this, he transforms Rodriguez's systematic and objective portrayal into a subjective, and at times passionate, satire with a strong moralistic tendency.[25]

Steinhöwel's greatest success was his *Esopus,* a bilingual compilation of ancient and medieval stories and fables of varying origin, none of them, however, by the Greek ex-slave Aesopus (620–560 B.C.) whose name the collection bears. In this work Steinhöwel proved himself not only a skillful translator but also a circumspect editor, offering, for instance, two different Latin versions in addition to the German translation for the first sixty fables. Illustrated with some two hundred woodcuts of extraordinary quality, the *Esopus* achieved instant fame. In Germany alone more than twenty editions appeared between 1477 and 1500. In addition, the Latin version without the German translation formed the basis for translations into French, English, and Dutch.

The observation, made earlier in this chapter, that the literature produced by Wyle, Steinhöwel, and Eyb is predominantly, although not exclusively, a literature of translations points to the limits but also to the strengths of early Humanism. There is no denying that this literature is largely derivative but it is also clear that it took German literature out of its provincialism and gave it a much-needed infusion of fresh ideas. But in addition to opening up a whole new repository of themes, stories, and motifs, the early Humanists contributed substantially to the formation of a new literary prose. There is, of course, a certain irony in the fact that it was not Wyle whose express goal had been to reform his native language but Eyb and Steinhöwel who had a much more lasting impact through their work.

In discussing early German Humanism it should be remembered that in no other period of German literature were the transitions between two ages so fluid as in the fifteenth century. Parallel to a broad stream of late medieval literature, a small current of Humanist writings began to appear from the middle of the century, gradually broadening and completely dominating the literary scene by the beginning of the sixteenth century. We should not forget, however, that these distinctions between medieval and Humanist are much clearer to the literary historian who operates with the benefit of hindsight than they were to the contemporary who, in most cases, was only vaguely, if at all, aware of them. Archduchess Mechthild, for example, supported with equal enthusiasm the romanticizing knightly epic poetry of a Hermann von Sachsenheim and the Humanist translations of Niclas von Wyle. Moreover, in some authors of that period, like Eyb and to a certain extent Steinhöwel, late medieval and Humanist mentalities coexisted peacefully. Keeping all this in mind, then, it is fair to say that the decade between 1450 and 1460 marks the beginning of early German Humanism: Eyb began writing his first Latin works in 1451, Luder started to lecture on the *studia humanitatis* at Heidelberg University in 1456, Wyle and Steinhöwel were launched on their modest literary careers, and small Humanist circles were beginning to form in various cities. If the middle of the century marks the beginning, the year 1480 can be called the end of that first phase of German Humanism. Within a few years the most important representatives of early Humanism died: Luder in 1472, Eyb in 1475, Steinhöwel in 1477, and Wyle in 1478. The very productive 1470s during which most of Humanist literature appeared were followed by the meagre 1480s, a time when hardly a work of note was written or published. By 1480 an important epoch of German literature had ended. The first generation of Humanists had died, and a new generation had yet to find its own way.

Chapter Three
Older Humanism

Jakob Wimpfeling

No other Humanist exemplified the tensions of his time more clearly than Jakob Wimpfeling. No one railed more vehemently against the abuses of the Church than he. Yet paradoxically he was a most devout Catholic. His views on the use of pagan classical authors in school were so narrow that they could have come from the most dogmatic Scholastic theologian. Yet, against the opposition of the monasteries, he forcefully demanded the establishment of the first secular *gymnasium* in Strasbourg. Moreover, with singular vividness and candor he described the exploitation and suffering of the peasants, but resignation and pious fortitude were the only remedies he dared to offer. Fiercely patriotic, he nevertheless, when pressured, easily yielded to the supranational authority of the Pope. Finally, although he was the first German to write a comedy after classical models and was the author of a history of his country using relatively modern methods, because of his pronounced conservatism, some scholars, even today, deny him the title "Humanist."

The contradictions and inconsistencies embodied by Wimpfeling not only characterize him but were symptomatic of a whole generation of men who were taking cognizance of the Classics but, unwilling or unable to free themselves from medieval traditions, had not committed themselves completely to Humanism. To indicate the middle position that these authors occupy between Scholasticism and Humanism, the term *Scholastic Humanism* is frequently employed. Since it already suggests a prejudicial characterization, the neutral term *Older Humanism* will be used here to describe the lives and works of three representatives of that generation: Wimpfeling himself, Sebastian Brant, and Rudolf Agricola.

Jakob Wimpfeling was born, the son of a saddler, in 1450, in the old imperial Alsatian city of Schlettstadt (today Sélestat) which had the distinction of housing one of the best schools in southwest Germany.[1] Founded in the middle of the fifteenth century and financed by the city, this *Lateinschule* had as its first principal the Westphalian scholar Ludwig Dringenberg, who had brought with him the methods and ideals of the Brethren of the Common Life. After attending this school, Wimpfeling, at age fourteen, enrolled at the University of Freiburg, where he became the student and friend of Johannes Geiler of Kaysersberg. According to his own remorseful testimony, Wimpfeling led an immoral life in Freiburg. The only evidence of this is a number of love poems, some of them frankly obscene. Never printed, they are now safely locked up in the university library of Basel in Switzerland. Wimpfeling was promoted to the baccalaureate in 1466, stayed another two years in Freiburg, and then left that city because of the plague. His subsequent sojourn at the University of Erfurt was brief; but it was here that he had the experience that profoundly affected his life. Struck by a sign in a church saying "Noli peccare. Deus videt" ("Do not sin. God watches"), Wimpfeling resolved henceforth to mend his ways and lead a moral and God-fearing existence. Throughout his life he adhered to this resolution.

The next fourteen years were spent at the University of Heidelberg where Humanism hardly had made any inroads since Peter Luder had bravely tried to introduce it in the late 1450s. Here the great debates were not yet between the Humanists and Scholastics but between the Realists and Nominalists. The former claimed that universals have a reality independent of the action of the mind, while the latter favored the view that individual things alone are real apart from the mind, and universality can be explained only as a function of the mental power to classify whereby words have a reference to the particulars which are the members of a class. These disputes were conducted with all the passion of youth. Each camp championed its own professors, fights broke out frequently, and to prevent further clashes, the nominalistically and realistically minded students were housed in different buildings. Wimpfeling seems to have kept himself aloof from these academic quarrels while rapidly climbing the academic ladder. After being promoted to Master of Arts in 1471, he studied canon law, and then theology. Receiving his baccalaureate in theology in 1478, he became Dean of the Faculty of Arts in 1480 and Rector of the University one year later.

Of the numerous works written by Wimpfeling during this period only his comedy *Stylpho* has managed to occupy a niche in almost all literary histories.[2] In March 1480, he participated as Dean in the awarding of the licentiate degrees. Departing from the tradition of delivering a *laudatio* on the freshly promoted graduates, Wimpfeling recited, or had recited, a text that today is considered the first comedy of German Humanism. The dramatic impetus derives from the confrontation of two young men: Stylpho, who in spite of his ignorance has been able to secure a number of benefices and expectancies during his long stay at the Roman Curia, and Vincentius, a poor but hard-working student who hopes to earn his living in an honest way. To settle the dispute about their different approaches to life, they go to the village priest Lampertus, who only underscores Stylpho's sentiments: "Scholarship does not fill the pockets. University studies are useless, only Rome rewards you."[3] Still, Stylpho, who would like to have a parish, has first to pass an examination administered by his former teacher Petrucius. In this burlesque examination scene—certainly the highlight of the little drama—Stylpho is shown as a total failure so that he is sent back by his examiner to the bishop, where he is informed that his career in this diocese has come to an end. Disappointed, he goes to the mayor of his native city to ask for the position of sexton which reportedly has become vacant. But since this opening has just been filled, the mayor offers him another position, even though there are a number of other qualified applicants. Stylpho, however, the much-traveled man who even has been to Rome, is given preference. The job is that of the village swineherd. Vincentius, on the other hand, the poet tells us, can look forward to a splendid career in the Church. To be sure, the plot of the comedy is simple and the suspense bearable. Yet these deficiencies are balanced by the quick flow of the Latin prose and the sharpness of the satire directed against the accumulation of benefices, the immorality of the Roman Curia, and the ignorance of the clergy.

The plague put an end to Wimpfeling's activities in Heidelberg. Students and professors had to leave the picturesque town on the Neckar. Wimpfeling was offered the position of cathedral preacher in Speyer—a somewhat surprising offer considering his delicate health and his own fears that his voice might not project in the large building. Though it is likely that he performed the duties of this office only for a short time, he could apparently live comfortably on the modest income associated with it. His scholarly leisure was interrupted only by a trip to his friend Trithemius, abbot of the monastery in Sponheim, who at Wimpfeling's suggestion, had earlier written a catalog of famous German men of letters.

Wimpfeling's literary activities in Speyer bore the stamp of his versatility. Although he was active in such diverse fields as literature, church history, and politics, his most important work written at that time was his educational treatise entitled *Isidoneus Germanicus* [Guide to the German youth]. Not knowledge *per se* is what Wimpfeling was primarily interested in but an education that stresses moral and ethical aspects. This aim not only implies high moral requirements on the part of the teacher, but also the inclusion of religious instruction which, for Wimpfeling, was synonymous with moral education. As far as the actual method is concerned, Wimpfeling advocated a simplification of the material and stress on the important aspects. Reading was to be emphasized at the expense of grammatical drills. The goal was competence in spoken and written Latin. To achieve it, the Alsatian educator recommended the reading of pagan authors, rejecting emphatically the one-sided condemnation of these authors by some theologians. Without a knowledge of these pagan authors, Christian writers, he maintained, are difficult or impossible to understand. Suitable according to Wimpfeling were: Virgil, Lucan, Horace (except the *Odes*), Plautus, Terence, Cicero, Sallust, Seneca, and the Roman historian Valerius Maximus. As we will see later on, this list is considerably longer and more inclusive than the one that he proposed later in his pamphlet against Jakob Locher. Still, even at that time, the number of authors on his index of forbidden books included Juvenal, Ovid, Persius, Martial, Tibullus, Propertius, Catullus, and Sappho, whom, incidentally, he considered to be a Latin poetess.

Moved by repeated readings of Petrarch's *De vita solitaria* [Solitary life], Wimpfeling decided to remove himself from the world and lead the life of a recluse in the Black Forest. But these plans were thwarted by Elector Philipp who wanted to institute a course of poetry at the University of Heidelberg and who called on the famous scholar's expertise to initiate such a program. In 1498 Wimpfeling therefore returned to his old university and lectured on Prudentius and Saint Jerome. In addition to two works dealing with the education of princes dedicated to his benefactor Philipp and the latter's oldest son, he wrote what is probably his most significant pedagogical work, the *Adolescentia* [Youth].[4]

In our modern sense the *Adolescentia* can hardly be called an original work. As a matter of fact, Wimpfeling himself lists at the beginning fifty authors he claims to have imitated and whose ideas he quotes, ranging from Plato to Sebastian Brant and from Socrates to Enea Silvio Piccolomini—in other words, from antiquity to the present. But Wimpfeling was not a slavish copyist. His originality lay in the arrangement of these quotations and in the way he shortened and supplemented them. This mixture of so many sources, however, may also be the reason why it is difficult to give an idea of this book since its organization is by no means clear. Instead of an argument progressing from A to B to C, we have an enumeration of often loosely connected ideas, suggestions, and pieces of advice presented in 105 chapters. Even such an intrepid Wimpfeling scholar as Otto Herding admitted that for the modern reader the *Adolescentia* is only bearable with a commentary. It goes without saying that Herding has provided us with such a commentary in addition to making an edition of Wimpfeling's work.

The tract begins with what Herding calls a psychological typology (*psychologische Typenlehre*), a description of six good and bad predispositions or tendencies in the young man. The positive ones are: largesse, hope, magnanimity, lack of suspicion, pity, and shame. The negative ones: concupiscence, inconsistency, credulity, irascibility, lying, lack of moderation. The latter are those maladies against which a teacher has to administer remedies in the same way a physician prescribes medicine. This is followed by a group of chapters dealing with the father-son relationship which, in turn, is followed by chapters devoted to thoughts on the fleetingness of life and on the *vita activa* and *vita contemplativa*. In the ensuing sections Wimpfeling voices strong objections against hunting, robbery of church property, and unjust wars. A chapter on death concludes the book. Empirical moralist that he was, Wimpfeling had a penchant for concreteness, wasting little time in abstract speculation, offering instead a colorful mosaic of useful advice, including suggestions on how to resist temptations of the flesh or why one should not curl one's hair. Such practice, he warns, makes a woman out of a man, unnerves youth, weakens the brain, excludes him from heaven and—offers a refuge to bugs.[5]

Whatever the shortcomings of the *Adolescentia* from a modern point of view, at the beginning of the sixteenth century it was a great success. Printed eight times between 1500 and 1505—later editions starting with that of 1505 contained additions by Wimpfeling's student and friend Johannes Gallinarius—it became the pedagogical gospel of German Humanism right up to the beginning of the Reformation.

In 1501 Wimpfeling left Heidelberg and went to Strasbourg. No doubt he was attracted to this city by two friends, Johannes Geiler von Kaysersberg, who had been cathedral preacher there since 1478, and Sebastian Brant, who had gone there at the invitation of Geiler to assume the post of legal adviser. Following Wimpfeling's arrival, these three formed the nucleus of a literary society in Strasbourg which, though thriving commercially, was by no means the intellectual center it ought to have been as the largest city in Alsace. Although Heidelberg, for example, had had a university since 1386, Basel since 1459, Freiburg since 1475, and although even the much smaller Schlettstadt had a *Lateinschule,* Strasbourg could not boast of such learned institutions. Beyond a number of privately organized elementary schools it housed several schools associated with the town's monasteries and convents.

This is the background of Wimpfeling's *Germania.*[6] Dedicated to the city council of Strasbourg in 1501, it contains, among other things, a proposal for the establishment of a secular, community-sponsored school. It is a curious work consisting of two loosely connected parts. In the first and shorter section Wimpfeling tried to prove that Alsace had been inhabited by Germans since the time of Emperor Augustus and that it had always belonged to the Empire. Documenting his thesis by a host of arguments, some sound, others unconvincing and naïve, Wimpfeling explained that he was prompted to write this work by rumors that certain fellow citizens were sympathizing with the French. Living in a province which, because of its proximity to France, was vulnerable to French annexationalist policies, the patriotic Humanist attempted to refute, once and for all, any claims the French might have had on the left bank of the Rhine in this area.

Although in the first part of the *Germania,* Wimpfeling, the German patriot speaks, it is the Humanist and educator who has the word in the second. In his usual rambling manner he develops his ideas on the preconditions and basic principles of a well-ordered state, with various comments on social, pedagogical, and theological questions added for the enlightenment of the good city fathers of Strasbourg. Embedded in these comments is his proposal for the establishment of a *gymnasium* (*Fechtschule,* as he calls it), which—and that is the new Humanist element—was meant as a general preparatory school for secular professions, such as notaries, merchants, administrators, and military leaders. The treatise ends with an effusive praise of Strasbourg, which he claims has only one rival: Rome itself. The city councillors graciously accepted Wimpfeling's *Germania,* whose title was scarcely appropriate for the first part and totally inappropriate for the second, and showed their appreciation by giving him the considerable sum of twelve florins. As for the *Fechtschule,* on that they deferred action.

Patriotism had prompted him to write the *Germania;* it also inspired him to his next work, the *Epitome Rerum Germanicarum,* freely translated as *A Short History of Germany,* in which he traced the development of his country from the earliest times to the present. While his chapters on ancient times are full of fables and legends, a number of more reliable sources such as annals and chronicles were consulted for the Middle Ages. Starting with Charlemagne, Wimpfeling's history follows the succession of the emperors, culminating in a praise of Maximilian. It is remarkable that not only the military and political background is treated but also the cultural history, so that this book becomes a veritable hall of fame of German philosophers, theologians, poets, musicians, historians, architects, sculptors, and painters. Under the heading "De pictura et plastica," for instance, we have the first literary mention of Albrecht Dürer. Wimpfeling's aim is to prove that the Germans need not have any inferiority complexes vis-à-vis other countries. As usual, his patriotism is coupled with a dislike of foreigners, in this case the Swiss, who had rebelled against the empire, and of course the French. There are other short-comings. Wimpfeling uncritically accepts the authority of the ancient writers; the composition is haphazard, and the moralizing pronounced. Yet considering the fact that historiography was still in its infancy in Germany, this first systematic history of the German lands is an extraordinary work which contributed to the development of a German national historiography.

It is a tragic fact that Wimpfeling, who loved the peace of his study and who, more than once, considered becoming a hermit, got embroiled repeatedly in time-consuming and nerve-racking feuds.

In 1505 he collided in rapid succession with the Augustinians, the Swabians, and the Swiss. Unedifying as these quarrels may have been, they all paled in comparison with Wimpfeling's controversy with Jakob Locher—a controversy that went far beyond the quarrel of two vain and irritable scholars but marked the break between the older Humanists and younger scholars who were bolder in their use of pagan classical antiquity. Increasingly, the literary world in Germany was split into two camps: on the one hand, the lay writers and secular poets, and on the other, the theologians and monks. This schism was subsequently to reach its highest pitch in the controversy between Reuchlin and the Dominicans of Cologne. The Locher-Wimpfeling debate, however, was a prelude to that more famous feud. Since it throws into sharp relief the tensions tearing apart the intellectual community at the beginning of the sixteenth century, it will be related here in some detail.

After studies in Italy and Basel, Jakob Locher became professor of rhetoric in Ingolstadt in 1498—an occasion he had celebrated by the ringing of all the church bells in that city. His translation of Brant's *Narrenschiff* [Ship of fools] into Latin (cf. p. 48), his edition of Horace (the first in Germany), and his own poems explain the high reputation he enjoyed in Humanist circles. He soon became involved in an argument with a colleague from the theological faculty, Georg Zingel, who expressed the traditional opinion that ancient pagan literature was only a means to an end and that it had to be subordinated to theology. Locher fired off an angry pamphlet accusing Zingel of being an ignorant fanatic, a viper, and ferocious animal who had been born before the deluge of a woman and the devil, concluding his diatribe with a bad pun: "Requiescat in pice" ("may he rest in pitch").[7] The object of these flatteries, Georg Zingel, had, in the meantime, enlisted the help of his old friend Wimpfeling and the latter's student Thomas Wolf, who posted a few epigrams against Locher on the bulletin board of the University of Freiburg whence Locher had recently retreated. Locher retaliated by doing the same against Wimpfeling and Wolf. Just as in the 1960s and 1970s the ideological battles between leftists and conservatives in the same university were often fought with large wall newspapers, here the feud was carried on with libelous epigrams, until the rector of the university intervened, banning the posting of further satires. Deeply hurt, Wimpfeling returned to Strasbourg, from where he wrote a letter to Locher admonishing him to mend his ways—an exhortation which was answered by a new barrage of abuse.

In the meantime, the respected jurist Ulrich Zasius, another of Wimpfeling's friends, decided to give lectures on those classics that were less suspect of subverting young minds, delivering them at the very same hour when Locher expounded on Ovid. Enraged by this childish rivalry, Locher reopened the skirmish with a series of epigrams directed against his scholastic competitors; the foe soon answered by similar rejoinders. The quarrel became more and more personal. One day, when leaving the university, the two scholars showered verbal abuse upon each other in the middle of the street for a whole hour. Locher accused Zasius of forbidding students to attend his rival's lectures, while Zasius responded that it is much better to attend an honest explication of Plautus—an author he happened to lecture on—than to listen to obscene and lascivious fables. The tempestuous Locher was put under house arrest and finally asked to leave Freiburg. He returned to Ingolstadt and resumed his lectures—this time without the accompaniment of ringing church bells. Revenging himself for his ignominious exit from Freiburg, however, he wrote a pamphlet whose satire is matched only by its bawdiness. It is both a defense of poetry and a virulent attack on theology and theologians whose parentage is explained as follows:

> Mula aliquid gignit; quid stercora foeda, quid inde?
>   Theologus crudus nascitur atque loquax.
>
> (A she-mule brings forth something. What? Loathsome excrements.
>   What after that?
>   An immature and loquacious theologian is born.)[8]

The days of chivalry were definitely over.

If Wimpfeling, who, after all, was a professional theologian, was embittered, he did not show it. At least not for a while, for his pamphlet *Contra turpem libellum Philomusi defensio Theologiae* [Defense of theology against the infamous book of Philomusus] did not appear until 1510. Apart from the expected attacks on his opponent, whom he calls alternately monkey, donkey, and pig, the book is a wholesale condemnation of the pagan poets and poetry itself, and an unabashed defense of Scholasticism and theology. Poets are useless, he says.

They only recite fables, absurdities, and obscenities. Has not God himself brought punishment on them? Euripides, for example, was mauled by dogs. Terence died in a shipwreck, Lucan was poisoned, Homer died of chagrin. Sophocles on the other hand, Wimpfeling argues with impeccable logic, died of having triumphed in a literary competition. The muses are the daughters of Jupiter, and Jupiter is the devil. Therefore the muses are also devils.

This treatise against Locher has often been cited as proof that Wimpfeling was an arch-conservative, narrow-minded Scholastic who actively opposed Humanism. This assessment would be correct if this were the only work he ever wrote. But it is important to take the situation into consideration. He had been mercilessly attacked, and his profession ridiculed. Feeling that he had been boxed into a corner, he got carried away. If one, therefore, considers these circumstances as well as his other works, a man emerges who was a Humanist, but a timid one perhaps, one who was easily frightened and plagued by religious scruples. To be sure, this tepid Humanism contrasts sharply with that of Locher and his followers. Theirs was a bold, aggressive kind that saw the beauty of the Latin language and literature as something valuable in itself and not only as an instrument for reading Christian authors.

Yet the same Wimpfeling who so loudly denounced almost all classical authors also headed the Strasbourg literary society; when Erasmus, the prince of Humanism, stopped over in Strasbourg on his way to Basel in 1514 a banquet was given in his honor. After the guest's departure, Wimpfeling wrote to him on behalf of his group, bidding the celebrated Humanist once more a cordial farewell, and kindly asking him for a letter in response.[9] In his long reply from Basel Erasmus thanked his hosts for the friendly reception he had been given in the "pearl of Alsace," praising Wimpfeling and his fellow Strasbourgians in the most flattering terms.[10]

In 1515 Wimpfeling withdrew to his native city of Schlettstadt where he gathered a few young people around himself, forming a literary society on the model of that of Strasbourg. To his dismay he soon saw that the young generation had increasingly emancipated itself from the restraints of the Church. One after the other, the works of the pagan authors whom he had condemned so passionately in his anti-Locher pamphlet appeared in print in Strasbourg.

The same feeling of being left behind must also have struck him when the Reformation came to Alsace. To be sure, his first reaction was one of enthusiasm, for no one had deplored the abuses of the Church more sharply than he. Yet when he saw the Reformation in its larger dimensions, realizing that it implied not only the abolition of clerical abuses but also radical changes in dogmatic and liturgical matters, he refused to follow. To his great disappointment, many of his students declared themselves in favor of the new church, among them Johann Sturm, one of his favorites and later a very influential educational reformer in Strasbourg. When Wimpfeling reproached him for being a heretic, Sturm answered "If I am a heretic it is you who made me one."[11] Left by his friends, embittered, alone, and sick, the man who had been known from the Alps to the Frisian islands spent his last years in Schlettstadt where he died on November 15, 1528.

Sebastian Brant

Sebastian Brant is chiefly remembered today as the author of the *Narrenschiff* [Ship of fools, 1494]. No other German book before Goethe's *Werther* (1774) was such a success at home and abroad. Numerous translations and adaptations appeared in quick succession, giving it the status of an early European best seller. It spawned a major literary genre, the *Narrenliteratur,* the literature of fools, and also gave birth to a minor genre, *Grobianismus* or grobianic literature. In our own times Katherine Anne Porter was inspired by the German Humanist to call one of her novels *The Ship of Fools* (1962), although the story itself, an account of a voyage from Veracruz to Bremerhaven in 1931 on the German ship *Vera,* has little to do with Brant's revue of fools.

Unfortunately, Brant's fame as the author of the *Narrenschiff* has overshadowed his reputation as a Latin author, poet, historian, editor, and jurist. A brief look at his biography as well as his other important works will help us to appreciate his intellectual breadth and versatility.

Brant was born in Strasbourg in 1457. Little is known about his childhood except that he probably attended the parish school of St. Thomas and later a school in Baden. In 1475 he enrolled at the University of Basel, was awarded the baccalaureate degree in 1477, and then decided to study law, receiving his license to teach and practice jurisprudence in 1484.[12]

Nowhere north of the Alps were the conditions for Humanism so favorable as in Basel. Some fifty years earlier, during the Church council (1431–1449), this city, as was noted before, had provided the opportunities for first contacts between Italian Humanists and their German admirers. Since the founding of the university in 1460, Humanist studies had been pursued here, first mostly by wandering poets like Peter Luder, Johann Mathias von Gengenbach, and Jakob Zimmermann, later by regular salaried professors. Nascent Humanism had been given a welcome boost by the arrival of Johann Heynlein von Stein and Johann Reuchlin. This was the intellectual climate Brant found when he arrived in Basel. Quickly he struck up friendships with both men; encouraged and inspired by the slightly older Reuchlin, he plunged into Humanist studies. After the example of other Humanists, he gave himself a Latin name, Titio, and from 1484 regularly offered courses on Latin authors. One of his students during that time was Jakob Locher, the future translator of his *Narrenschiff* into Latin, who had only the highest praise for his teacher, saying that Brant introduced the youth into the "charming sanctuary of true poetry." Another student wrote from Cologne, where he had moved in the meantime, that he was envious of Basel for its cultivation of literary studies, while in Cologne "nobody knew how to gladden the hearts with Latin verse."

While Brant thus gladdened the hearts of his students with Latin verse, he was not sufficiently distracted by the *studia humanitatis* to neglect his legal studies which he successfully completed with the promotion to Doctor of Law. It has been suggested that poetry was his first love and that he only embarked on the more solid legal career out of the necessity of maintaining a family. This view disregards the deep satisfaction the study of law gave him, filling a need for order and discipline in his nature. He was especially attracted to Roman law, seeing in it a unifying factor in the hopelessly disunited German empire.

In addition to his work at the university as lecturer in poetry and professor of canon and civil law, Brant was also a practicing lawyer as well as a reader or editor for various printing houses in Basel. In this capacity his task was to aid the printers in the selection and editing of works as well as in the composition of dedications, prefaces, and colophons. Scholars suspect that the busy Humanist was involved in the editing of about one third of the books published in Basel in the last decades of the fifteenth century. Though proofreading and the constant preoccupation with legal matters were hardly conducive to the writing of poetry, Brant also composed a considerable number of poems during that time, at first mostly in Latin, later increasingly in the vernacular.

In 1485 he married Elisabeth Burg. Of the seven children from this marriage, Brant's oldest son, whom he gave the unusual name Onophrius after his favorite saint, was the particular object of his Humanist ambitions. Brant taught him Latin when he was a mere child and enrolled him at the University of Basel at age seven. Nevertheless, Onophrius did not fulfill the high hopes his father had placed in him. He later got a subordinate position in the Strasbourg city administration and wrote some poetry—in German.

Several factors prompted Brant to leave Basel and return to his native Strasbourg in 1501. In that year Basel, which, up to that time, had been a free imperial city, joined the Swiss Confederation. Such a move was a bitter disappointment to Brant, whose main political concern had ever been the unity and preservation of the German empire. But this was hardly the sole reason. Another factor in his choice was the perfectly understandable desire to return to the city where he had been born and where his family and many of his friends lived. Finally, the wish to exchange the triple burden of professor, practicing lawyer, and editor for one well-paid position certainly also played a role in his decision to accept the post of legal adviser to the city of Strasbourg. Quickly winning the respect of his fellow citizens, he was promoted after three years to the position of municipal secretary *(Stadtschreiber)*. His duties included serving as a lawyer to the council, acting as editor of minutes of the council meetings, conducting the correspondence, and censoring all publications appearing in the city.

Two events in these Strasbourg years throw an interesting light on Brant's mentality and help to define his position within the large spectrum of German Humanism. The first concerns his involvement in the Locher-Zasius-Wimpfeling controversy, the second his attitude in the Reuchlin affair. In addition to having written enthusiastic letters about his former teacher, Jakob Locher had also translated Brant's *Narrenschiff*. A genuine friendship between these two men had developed. For these reasons alone one might have expected Brant to align himself with Locher in this quarrel. But the latter's attacks on theology and Scholasticism, his unabashed defense of the classics went too far for Brant's conservative bent of mind. He therefore decided to support Zasius, at least clandestinely, supplying him with a few choice anti-Locher epigrams, which constituted, as will be recalled, the main ammunition in that unsavory controversy. Being a cautious lawyer, however, Brant asked Zasius under no circumstances to reveal the identity of the author of these verses.[13]

The second event that helps us place Brant on the cultural map of German Humanism is his complete silence in the controversy between Reuchlin and the Dominicans of Cologne (cf. p. 76). Fellow students at the University of Basel, Brant and Reuchlin had been associated in a cordial and at times intimate friendship through the years. Writing to him in 1500, Brant addressed Reuchlin as: "My sweet Capnion [Reuchlin's Latinized name], my brother who is dearer to me than life."[14] But when the "sweet Capnion" repeatedly begged Brant for some encouraging words, the latter, who otherwise maintained a lively correspondence with a host of men, kept an icy silence. This cruel aloofness seems even stranger in light of the fact that both shared the same enemies, the German Dominicans. Yet the difference was as revealing as it was important. Brant attacked the Dominicans because they did not believe in the immaculate conception of the Virgin Mary, a doctrine he staunchly defended. The Reuchlin feud, on the other hand, was not primarily a theological disagreement but revolved around the question of whether Humanists should be restricted by the Church in their scholarly work. Brant's failure to take a stand, however, should not be interpreted to mean that he was no Humanist. During his years in Strasbourg he engaged in such thoroughly Humanist pursuits as editing classical authors and taking a lively part in the literary activities of the Strasbourg literary society.

Toward the end of his life Brant became increasingly pessimistic. Several times he believed he saw signs of great catastrophes in the planets. Two further events aggravated this pessimism: the Reformation, the scope and importance of which he did not and could not understand, and the death in 1519 of Emperor Maximilian, a man in whom he had placed the highest hopes for a strong empire and a crusade against the Turks. In 1520, at age sixty-three, Brant undertook the arduous journey to Ghent, heading the Strasbourg delegation to pay homage to the new Emperor Charles V. One year later, on May 10, 1521, he died.

In his by no means complete bibliography of Brant's writings Charles Schmidt lists seventy-two items.[15] Not only the quantity but also the range and diversity of Brant's literary works is astonishing. He was an editor of Latin texts, the author of widely read legal works, an historian, a translator of Latin works, a publicist, a bilingual poet, and possibly a dramatist.

As the author of juridical works he zealously propagated Roman law, the introduction of which he hoped would lead to an improvement of legal conditions in the empire. His accomplishment as an historian is small compared with that of his friend Wimpfeling, consisting only of two works. His *Chronik über Deutschland, zuvor des lands elsass und der löblichen statt Strassburg* [Chronicle of Germany, especially Alsace and the praiseworthy city of Strasbourg], published only after his death and then incompletely, testifies not only to Brant's geographical and historical interests but also to his proud patriotism which he shared with Wimpfeling and other Alsatian Humanists. Interesting for the cultural historian is *Bischoff Wilhelms von Hoensteins waal und einrit anno 1506 und 1507* [Bishop Wilhelm of Hoenstein's election and entrance in the years 1506 and 1507]. Written with keen observation, humor, and surprising candor, it describes the election and festive entrance of the new bishop of Strasbourg. The promise, made in the work's subtitle, of giving a detailed description, is scrupulously kept. Reading in parts like a minute-by-minute eyewitness account of the events of the day, it also casts interesting sidelights on life at the beginning of the sixteenth century which are likely to dispel any romantic notions about the "good old times": boisterous and unruly crowds have to be dispersed by the police, the food is bad, the city council so parsimonious that Brant himself has to pay the messengers out of his own pocket. This work shows Brant at his best: concrete, lively, and humorous.

Brant began his poetic career with Latin poems, both religious and secular.[16] The majority of the religious poems were devoted to Mary and her cult. Brant sings the Virgin's praises, describes her feasts and the localities where she is worshipped. Twenty-three poems are devoted to various saints, among them Joachim, Mary's father, and Onophrius, who, as will be recalled, had a special place in Brant's heart.[17] Not all poems, however, deal with religious themes. There are some on current events, like the flood in Basel, on literary figures of the past like Roswitha von Gandersheim and Petrarch, addresses and dedications to friends like Johann Geiler von Kaysersberg, Johann Dalberg, Johann Heynlein von Stein, and of course Emperor Maximilian. It is certainly odd, albeit pardonable, when Brant proudly parades his freshly acquired facility of writing Latin poetry. In his *Vita sanctissimi Onofrii* [Life of the most holy Onophrius], for instance, he pedantically identifies the meter of every single stanza beforehand. And his biographer Edwin H. Zeydel is right in poking gentle fun at this practice.[18]

As a publicist Brant was active through broadsides, one- or two-page pamphlets on topical issues, especially between 1488 and 1504. Often Latin and German versions, in most cases accompanied by a woodcut, appeared side by side. Apart from their obvious linguistic differences, these publications also differ in their thematic emphasis. While those written in the vernacular stress the moral-didactic element, the Latin ones shift the accent to political-juridical questions. Unusual phenomena, like floods, hailstorms, news of misfits, or historical events are described and often interpreted as portents of future events. Twenty of these broadsides are still extant.[19]

If some modern scholars are right, the designation "playwright" has to be added to Brant's impressive list of titles. For according to two rather vague statements made by Jakob Wimpfeling, Brant was involved in the production of a play called *Hercules at the Crossroads*, performed not long before the fall of 1512.[20] Though not specifically mentioned as the author, Brant has been considered as such since Charles Schmidt published his *Histoire littéraire de l'Alsace* in 1879. The drama itself has not yet been found. More recently, Dieter Wuttke has argued that the *Historia Herculis* (1515) by Pangratz Bernhaubt called Schwenter is the German version of a Latin drama by a certain Gregorius Arvianotorfes. The name Arvianotorfes, Wuttke maintains, was really a pseudonym for Brant.[21] The question has been further complicated by the discovery of the *Tugent-Spyl . . . Durch Doctor Sebastianum Brand in Reimens Weiss gestellet* [Play of virtue, rhymed by Doctor Sebastian Brant], which had been published by a certain Johann Winckel in Strasbourg in 1554, more than thirty years after Brant's death. Many questions, however, remain unresolved and the debate is still going on. Until further evidence is brought to light, the discussions will stay on the level of hypothesis and Brant the dramatist will remain an elusive figure.

Jakob Wimpfeling, who was always preoccupied with educational questions, wanted the *Narrenschiff* used as a textbook, Ulrich von Hutten claimed it was written with a new set of rules (*nova lege*), Trithemius called it a "divina satura," a divine satire, and Jakob Locher compared its author to Dante and Petrarch. This was high praise, even by the standards of the Humanists, who were exceedingly polite among themselves—unless, of course, they indulged in slandering each other. For us, this acclaim accorded to the *Narrenschiff* does not seem to be justified. Used to the variety and subtlety of German poetry of the last two centuries, we find Brant's verse crude and the composition haphazard. Furthermore, in a work which looks like an epic there is no plot. The motif of the ship's journey from Narbonne to Narragonia with its interesting narrative possibilities is dropped as soon as it is mentioned only to be taken up at the end of the work in a very cursory manner. Nor is there any discernible progression from minor foibles to cardinal sins. To be sure, since Brant spares no one, we get an almost total picture of German society at the end of the fifteenth century with fascinating sidelights on cultural and sociological aspects of that time. But is the *Narrenschiff* a work of art (as the Humanists claimed) that should be discussed in a survey of German Humanism?

The question of its artistic merit has to be deferred for a moment so that we can give a brief account of the contents of the *Narrenschiff*.[22] The fools and their follies are described in 112 separate chapters, each of them consisting of a three-line motto, a woodcut, and a text of varying length. After each fool is characterized, the argument against that particular folly is buttressed by a host of examples from the Bible and classical authors. Sparing no one, Brant parades before our eyes an almost endless variety of fools ranging from beggars to bishops and from peasants to princes. Major vices like greed, usury, adultery, and blasphemy are ridiculed just as forcefully as minor transgressions such as not keeping secrets or boasting. The tricks employed by beggars to display their pretended maladies are so vividly described that Mr. Peachum in Bertolt Brecht's *Dreigroschenoper* would become green with envy. That people turn away from God aroused Brant's anger just as much as the noise the faithful produce in church with their barking dogs, wing-flapping hawks, and clattering wooden shoes. Neither quack doctors nor sanctimonious priests escape Brant's satirical arrows. A colorful procession of lax parents, bibliophiles, gluttons, nymphomaniacs, procrastinators, dancers, gamblers, procurers, knights, and deceitful cooks and waiters crowds the ship.

The *Narrenschiff* was intended as a mirror for the fools themselves:

> For fools a mirror shall it be,
> where each his counterfeit may see.
> His proper value each would know,
> the glass of fools the truth may show.[23]

The opposite of folly, however, is wisdom *(wissheyt)*, and only those who are able to recognize themselves in this looking glass can find their way to wisdom:

> Whoever his foolishness decries
> alone deserves to rank as wise.[24]

The author's ultimate goal, then, is to lead the fool through self-recognition to wisdom. Not being a fool, but remaining one is considered reprehensible.

Behind the didactic intention certain ideals become visible. These are conservative and retrospective, such as the call for a return to divine laws or a restitution of the authority of Church and empire. In this respect Brant's thinking is medieval. But he also appears as the advocate of the new emerging middle-class ideology, characterized by an avoidance of extremes, a strong sense of community and self-respect, and a high regard for reason. Like Brant himself, his *Narrenschiff* is the product of a transitional period.

The vivid description and sheer variety of the fools, the use of the popular four-beat doggerel, and the folksy, concrete language—all this certainly accounts for the enormous success the book had with the German reading public. But it does not explain the high esteem the work enjoyed among such Humanists as Locher, Hutten, and Wimpfeling, who praised it not because of its subject matter but because of its formal literary aspects. Why should they, who were trained in the classics, acclaim a work that looked more or less like a casually arranged series of broadsides? At least this is the impression the modern reader gets. This seeming lack of composition was pointed out as early as 1854 by Zarncke,[25] whose assessment has been handed down from one generation of scholars to the next. Thus M. O'C. Walshe said in 1962: "In the *Narrenschiff* Brant showed himself totally incapable of organizing a narrative event to the extent of maintaining the most elementary consistency in the story."[26] But it is precisely the "organization of the narrative event" that the German scholar Ulrich Gaier has concentrated on in two pioneering studies on the *Narrenschiff*.[27]

Taking the Humanists' comments on Brant's masterpieces seriously, Gaier tried to prove that the Alsatian had created a rhetorically and artistically formed work of art—in other words, a truly Humanist work. The reason why this is not easily perceived today, argued Gaier, is that Brant was faced with the awesome task of wanting to appeal both to the middle class *and* his learned readers, two groups which were entirely different in schooling, logical training, and linguistic facility. The sententiousness of the work, its concrete descriptions, and pithy sayings were intended for bourgeois readers, while the allusions to the Bible and classical authors could be savored by the more learned. To them the careful structure of each chapter might also become transparent. In addition to deliberately organizing individual chapters, Brant grouped clusters of them into thematic complexes. These motifs are taken up, dropped, and yet woven into complicated patterns, discernible only to those trained in the art of ancient rhetoric. There is also, according to Gaier, a progression toward the last chapters, climaxing in a strong appeal to recognize one's foolishness and return to wisdom. The whole work, then, Gaier argues, was planned as a coherent unity and executed with meticulous care as a hortatory speech, a *suasoria,* built on long-established rhetorical principles.

Gaier further makes the point that the *Narrenschiff* is essentially a revival of the ancient form of satire. Carefully comparing Brant's work with that of the great Roman satirists, Horace, Persius, and Juvenal, he maintains that a satire is characterized by a candid depiction of reality and a will to improve the weaknesses of men. By that definition Brant certainly was a satirist, for he wanted to rouse fools from their complacency, confront them with a mirror, and help them to shed their follies, whatever they might have been. The *Narrenschiff,* then, is not an epic poem—a classification that, for a long time, has led to misunderstandings and false expectations. Rather it is a consciously organized *satire* and was understood as such by Brant's contemporaries.

The literary impact of the *Narrenschiff* was enormous. Between 1494 and 1512 six authorized editions were published. At the same time, much to Brant's chagrin, pirated editions appeared in various German cities. Adaptations and imitations also came out in quick succession. German literature of the sixteenth century thus became to an appreciable degree the history of the reception of the *Narren-schiff*, creating a genre which flourished as late as the eighteenth century. Johann Geiler von Kaysersberg, for instance, based 147 sermons on individual chapters of Brant's book; Thomas Murner was inspired to write his highly successful *Narrenbeschwörung* [Fools' exorcism], and Erasmus von Rotterdam drew inspiration from this work in his *Praise of Folly*. Similarly, Hans Sachs, the prolific Meistersinger of Nuremberg, eagerly plundered the *Narrenschiff* for material.

The impact of the book can also be gauged by the number of translations it inspired. The earliest and most influential in the long run was done by Jakob Locher into Latin (1497). The *Stultifera Navis*, as it was called, is more polished and elegant than its German original. While the latter scurries along in somewhat short-winded doggerel, the Latin version flows elegantly in the longer dactylic hexameter of the classic epic. Since Latin was the international language at the time, it was Locher's rendering that became the basis for French, English, and Dutch versions.[28] Frequently, the work went through many transmutations, and it takes a literary detective to unravel the complicated stemma. A case in point is Henry Watson's English prose version of 1509 which has proven to be a literal translation of the second edition of Drouyn's French prose version of 1499. This, in turn, was a reworking of the efforts in verse by Pierre Rivière (1497) which had been based on Locher's Latin adaptation of Brant's German original. It is a relief to learn that the translation into Low German was directly based on Brant's very own work.

Rudolf Agricola

"He could have been the first in Italy if he had not preferred Germany."[29] That was Erasmus's appraisal of Agricola; and considering the undisputed superiority of Italian letters at the time it was the highest commendation a German could receive. Calling him a man of great erudition and wide reading in Latin and Greek literature, Erasmus also praised Agricola as an excellent stylist worthy of being compared with Quintilian. With rare unanimity, virtually all later German Humanists echoed these sentiments. Nor was Agricola's fame confined to Germany. In 1530 the members of the Faculty of Theology in Paris accused their colleagues in the Faculty of Arts of studying Agricola more that Aristotle—a most serious charge in view of the unchallenged reign the Greek philosopher had enjoyed for centuries. Five years later, in 1535, and fifty years after Agricola's death, Henry VIII of England decreed that all students at Cambridge University should study Agricola in addition to Aristotle and Melanchthon. Even Italian scholars, who usually looked down with disdain on anything coming from the North, paid tribute to the German Humanist.[30]

That universal acclaim might come as a surprise for us today, since we are accustomed to basing a scholar's reputation on his literary output. But that was fairly modest in Agricola's case. He wrote little and published less; in a publish-or-perish climate he would have perished. A number of speeches, some translations from Greek into Latin, a handful of poems, some fifty letters, and one work on rhetoric—that is all we have from him.

It was thus not an impressive literary oeuvre but his personality— and one work published long after his death—that accounted for the general admiration he enjoyed. A look at his life and the environment that shaped him is therefore even more necessary than in other cases.

In the same year (1444) in which Enea Silvio wrote his novella *De Euriolo et Lucretia,* Rudolf Agricola (Roelof Huusman) was born in the small village of Baflo near Groningen, Frisia, which at that time belonged to the German Empire.[31] He was the offspring of a maidservant and a parish priest. Agricola's mother subsequently married a widower in whose house the young boy grew up. After attending St. Martin's school in Groningen, he enrolled, at age twelve, at the University of Erfurt. Cologne and Louvain, where he was awarded the master of arts degree with distinction, were the next stations of his academic wanderings. Using his stay in a French-speaking country to his linguistic advantage, he learned to speak and write French. In Louvain he also became increasingly interested in Cicero, Quintilian, and other Latin authors. And it was probably this new interest in the writers of classical antiquity and the prospect of studying them with competent teachers that prompted him to journey to Italy in 1468. He stayed in this country, with extended interruptions in 1470/71 and 1474, for over ten years—longer than any other German Humanist except Albrecht von Eyb. This decade, from his mid-twenties to his mid-thirties, was undoubtedly the decisive period of his intellectual development. First going to Pavia,

he soon abandoned legal studies and turned more and more to the
studia humanitatis, enthusiasm for which he shared with his friends
Johann von Dalberg, his later benefactor in Heidelberg, and the
brothers Dietrich and Johann von Pleningen. Having acquired a
reputation as an excellent speaker, he was repeatedly asked to deliver
the annual inauguration speech for the rectors of the scholars (*rectores
scholarium*). Attracted by its fame as a distinguished school for classical studies, Agricola transferred in 1474 to the University of Ferrara where, according to the wishes of its founders and benefactors,
the d'Este family, a strong liberal arts curriculum had been established in lieu of a profession-oriented program. Here famous teachers
like Theodorus Gaza, Tito Vespasiano Strozzi, and Battista Guarino,
the son of the even more famous Guarino of Verona, taught. Guided
by these scholars, the young German immersed himself completely
in the study of literature. In addition, he translated from Greek,
copied all of Quintilian, and supported himself by playing the organ
in the ducal chapel. In 1479 he returned to Germany. After brief
stays in Speyer and Cologne, he accepted the post of city secretary
in Groningen—a job he intensely disliked. In 1481 he was offered
the position of court secretary and future educator of the princes at
the Burgundian court, and two years later he was asked to become
the principal of the city school in Antwerp. He declined both offers,
citing his love of an unfettered existence and his longing for
independence.

During that time his old friend Johann von Dalberg, who in the
meantime had become chancellor of the Elector in Heidelberg and
Bishop of Worms, sent him an invitation to join him in the city
on the Neckar. Only after receiving Dalberg's repeated assurances
that he would have total freedom and no teaching obligations did
Agricola decide to move to Heidelberg. Though unconstrained by
any official duties at the university, he took an active part in academic affairs, delivering lectures and participating in the verbal
battles and disputations. Judging from the accounts of students, he
quickly became what today might be termed a "star professor,"
impressing his listeners not only with his refined Latin diction, but
also with his profound knowledge of ancient history and literature
as well as his noble and charming personality, so that students and
professors alike flocked to his lectures. Often, when others faltered
during a disputation, he clarified the issues by expounding such
difficult topics as the nature of fate, causality, and the immortality

of the soul. Elector Philipp, who loved and admired him and whose guest at Heidelberg castle Agricola frequently was, occasionally asked him for advice in governmental affairs. At his request, Agricola wrote an outline of a world history based on the best ancient authors. This work, however, has disappeared.

In the summer of 1485 Agricola accompanied Johann von Dalberg to Rome to congratulate Pope Innocent VIII on his election. During his return trip the Humanist fell ill and died a month later in Heidelberg on October 27, 1485. He was only forty-one years old.

While Sebastian Brant had to wait for three hundred years for a biographer and Wimpfeling gave his autobiography the characteristic form of an apology *(excusatio)*, no fewer than five different *vitae* appeared within sixty years of Agricola's death.[32] These are not only evidence of his popularity but, having been written shortly after his death, also provide us with valuable source material about his life, so that we are unusually well informed, not only regarding the external circumstances of his existence but also about his likes and dislikes, strengths and weaknesses, character and appearance. Like the portraits of the time, these studies are rich in details, some significant, and others less so. They offer concrete examples of the discovery of the unique human being, the individual, so often cited as a major feature of Renaissance Humanism.

Emerging from these accounts is a personality of astonishing versatility, "a sort of minor Leonardo da Vinci."[33] Tall, handsome, with chestnut-brown hair and beautiful hands, Agricola was a good athlete who enjoyed fencing, stone-throwing, whirling the discus, and ball-playing. As a skillful painter and draughtsman he was particularly interested in portraiture, occasionally watching his subjects clandestinely in church. Equally talented in music, he played the organ, lute, and flute, was a creditable singer with a warm baritone voice, and also tried his hand at composition and musical theory. He even distinguished himself as an organ-builder and was reported to have been the first to construct such an instrument with a "vox humana" stop. Having already mastered a number of languages such as Latin, Greek, High German, Low German, French, and several Italian dialects, he began to study Hebrew in Heidelberg in order to be able to read the Old Testament in the original. His Latin was said to be so good that during his years in Italy he was asked on various occasions to give public addresses in that language, a remarkable accomplishment for a Northerner and something even the great Erasmus, no mean Latinist himself, did not dare to do for fear of being laughed at by the haughty Italians. Friendly in his relations with others, Agricola had a gift for striking up lifelong friendships and avoided the kind of polemics which other Humanists cherished so much. His strong sense of independence and freedom not only kept him from marrying but also prompted him to renounce promising careers in politics and academics.

To commemorate the centenary of Petrarch's death, Agricola composed a speech on the great Italian Humanist around 1473/74.[34] The source of this *Vita Petrarchae* [Life of Petrarch], as it is usually referred to, is a factual summary in Italian of the poet's life in the second edition of the *Rime Sparse* (1471), which itself was a condensation of the biographical outline in Italian written in the middle of the fourteenth century by either Piero Candido Decembrio or Francesco Filelfo. Agricola, however, expanded this account to twice its original length and in doing so injected numerous personal comments. It is this personal tone that makes this short biography of Petrarch, the first by a non-Italian, such an interesting document. For there was a deep spiritual kinship between these two men. Both, though pressured by their families to study law, turned to literature; both valued their independence and freedom: Petrarch declined to enter the honorable and financially rewarding service of the chancellery at the Curia in Avignon, and Agricola refused the equally honorable employment at the Burgundian court. Both liked to travel, with Agricola praising the Italian's wanderlust to defend his own restlessness. Both men, finally, decided at a mature age to devote themselves to sacred letters. In the speech itself Agricola eulogized Petrarch as the restorer of the *studia humanitatis*. This assessment was by no means new or original, for seventy years before Leonardo Bruni had made exactly the same claim for his countryman.[35] However, in the course of the fourteenth century, as the Italian Humanists had become more sophisticated and demanding, Petrarch's literary fortunes had waned. For his Italian contemporaries, therefore, Agricola's oration was probably no more than a casual reminder of a literary figure long outshone by other lights. For the German Agricola, on the other hand, the intellectual encounter with Petrarch was a genuine discovery.

This sense of discovery of the *studia humanitatis* and their restorer also found expression in a number of Agricola's works, among them his address *In laudem philosophiae et reliquarum artium* [In praise of philosophy and other arts] which he delivered in 1476 before Duke Ercole of Ferrara.[36] In a self-deprecating way Agricola wonders aloud "why of all people he, who was born near the ocean and on the outermost frontiers of the world, could hope to say something new and worthy of the refined Italian ears of his listeners."[37] Whether what he said was new and worthy of refined Italian ears is difficult to judge. By German standards at any rate it was quite new. For what Agricola developed here was a new concept of philosophy, stressing moral over speculative philosophy, a concept, furthermore, in which philosophy was defined as the "love of wisdom, that is love of knowledge of divine and human things, tied in with the quest for a well-ordered life.[38] The models and precepts for this "well-ordered life," however, were to be found in the writings of the ancient historians, poets, and orators. Not surprisingly, then, Agricola's speech became in large part a praise of the *studia humanitatis,* and in a wider sense a celebration of the human mind with its power to reach for the highest perfection.

Eight years later, in 1484, Agricola voiced similar views in a letter to his young friend Barbirianus who had expressed a desire to study under his guidance. Unable to oblige him in this respect, the German Humanist instead offered him some advice on the right organization of his studies in this document which became known under the title *De formando studio* [On the curriculum].[39] He proposes to answer two questions: first, which field of study to choose, and second, which method to study by. Unhesitatingly Agricola recommends philosophy as the only field worthy to be studied. But, as in his *In laudem philosophiae,* the concept of philosophy he has in mind is different from that current in Germany at that time. Emphatically rejecting the Scholastic disputations with their attempts to "solve riddles that have not found an Oedipus in the course of so many centuries," he divides philosophy into three interrelated areas: moral philosophy, the knowledge of things (*rerum cognitio*), and the art of expressing ideas. By this definition, knowledge drawn not only from the Bible and such acknowledged moralists as Cicero and Seneca but from virtually all ancient pagan writers will lead to the right conduct.

The inclusion of these authors shows how far ahead of his time Agricola was; it will be recalled that as late as 1510 Wimpfeling banned them from the curriculum. It also demonstrates how all-embracing Agricola's concept of philosophy was, for not only philosophy proper and literature but also geography, medicine, agriculture, architecture, and history are covered by this broad definition. Equally important for a Humanist is the third aspect: the art of expression or rhetoric. Once again, the models for excellent diction can primarily be found in ancient writers. It is with this more practical aspect of studying that the second part of Agricola's letter is concerned, offering helpful advice on careful reading, good retention of the material, and creative reproduction.

If the reputation Agricola enjoyed among his contemporaries was largely due to his winning and fascinating personality, his fame among later generations rested chiefly on the one major work he wrote, *De inventione dialectica* [On dialectical invention]. Until it was replaced in 1543 by the *Dialecticae partiones* [System of dialectics] of the French Humanist Petrus Ramus (1515–1572), it was the mose widely read work on logic of the time. Completed in 1479, it circulated in manuscript for more than three decades until it was printed for the first time in Louvain in 1515. Between 1538 and 1543, to give only one example, fifteen different editions appeared.[40] Similarly, the royal injunctions making Agricola mandatory reading at Cambridge University, as well as the professorial reproaches in Paris cited at the beginning of this section, referred to this book.

Modern critics have tried to explain the work's contents by proposing a variety of alternate titles for it. Lewis Spitz, for instance, suggested that in seventeenth-century England it might have been called "The Compleat Orator," while Walter Ong proposed the titles "What Boys Should Know about Discourse" or "Thought on Discourse and How to Teach it."[41] What both scholars imply is that the title is a misnomer and that what appears to be a work on philosophy is in fact a manual for rhetoric, with dialectics being understood in a very loose sense as the whole field of human discourse. As in Agricola's other works, the practical orientation of the book is striking. Impatient with the senseless hairsplitting, empty formalism, and perplexing subtlety of Scholasticism, the Frisian Humanist wanted to meet the real needs of students. While for the Scholastics this kind of intellectual occupation was an end in itself, for Agricola it had a practical purpose.

De inventione dialectica is divided into three books. In the first Agricola deals with the *loci,* or aspects for the treatment of themes. All in all, sixty-three *loci* are discussed, seventeen drawn from Cicero, twenty-two from the fourth-century Greek rhetorician Themisitius, and twenty-four from himself. Just as the hunter, Agricola argues, does not arbitrarily change his hunting grounds but waits for the game where he is sure of it, so the orator needs the systematic division of these themes in order to avail himself easily of them in his argumentation. In the second book the author discusses dialectics proper as the art of reasoning. Just as the best weapons are worthless unless one knows how to handle them, so the whole variety of the *loci* is useless if it is not arranged correctly. The third book, finally, deals with the emotional appeal of a speech. Like his oration on philosophy, this work ends with an emphatic praise of the human mind: "Prodigious, immense, and unbelievable is the power of the human mind."[42]

Agricola's implied attacks on Scholasticism, launched in the spirit of the Italian Renaissance, should not lead us into assuming that he was in any way opposed to Christianity and its dogma. As a matter of fact, his verses, although few in number and undistinguished as poetry, are largely religious in nature. Moreover, three speeches, all delivered in 1484/85—an address to the clergy of Worms on the dignity of the priestly calling, a homily on Christmas, and the already mentioned congratulatory oration on Pope Innocent's election—provide ample proof that he was, like most German Humanists, firmly anchored in the Christian faith. Yet, unlike Wimpfeling with his narrow-minded condemnation of much of classical literature, Agricola did not consider a devout Christian faith and a genuine enthusiasm for pagan antiquity incompatible. Although chronologically belonging to the generation of Wimpfeling and Brant, he was intellectually one generation ahead, for his true contemporaries were Reuchlin, Celtis, Mutianus, and Erasmus, a fact sensed by later Humanists when they reverently referred to him as the "Father of German Humanism."

Chapter Four

The Flowering of Humanism: The First Generation

Conrad Celtis

Among those who stood around Agricola's deathbed in Heidelberg in October, 1485, was a young man of twenty-six. Attracted by the Humanist's fame, he had gone there only a year before. During their brief acquaintance Agricola had taught him Greek and, more important, had introduced him to the *studia humanitatis*. He could hardly have dreamed that this young man, a peasant's son from Franconia, was later to become the first German poet laureate, a reformer of university studies, an accomplished poet, a proud and eloquent patriot, a skillful playwright, and the tireless motor behind the founding of Humanist organizations.[1]

Conrad Celtis belonged to the generation of men who saw the flowering of Humanism, which occurred in the first two decades of the sixteenth century. By that time the Reuchlin affair (cf.p.76) had solidified the Humanist ranks, the new movement had become firmly established at the universities and the secular and ecclesiastical courts, the most significant literary works were being written, and the Reformation had not yet monopolized the attention of the Germans. In 1507 Nikolaus Gerbellius wrote: "I congratulate myself often on living in this glorious century in which so many remarkable men have arisen in Germany." It cannot be the task of this survey to discuss all the scholars, schoolmen, men of letters, clergymen, and jurists who can lay claim, in some way or other, to the title *Humanist*. As in the previous chapters we must concentrate on the most significant figures.

Celtis was born in 1459 as Konrad Bickel, or Pickel, in the small village of Wipfeld on the river Main between Schweinfurt and Würzburg. An older brother, a monk in a nearby monastery, probably taught him Latin, but his father, a hard-working wine-grower insisted on his son's taking up the same work. Growing grapes was not a career young Bickel had in mind for himself, however. Tired of carrying the heavy baskets full of grapes down the vineyards near his native village, he ran away from home at age eighteen. A lumber raft first took him down the Main and Rhine to Cologne where he registered at the university in 1477.

Cologne University at that time was not exactly a bastion of Humanism. As a matter of fact, with its long and glorious tradition of Scholasticism—Albertus Magnus and Duns Scotus had taught and Thomas Aquinas had studied here—and with its dominating theological faculty it was one of the most conservative universities in Germany, such as later became the laughing stock of the entire Humanist community through the *Letters of Obscure Men*. No wonder, then, that Celtis was deeply disappointed. In a later poem to his Cologne friend Wilhelm Mommerloch he bitterly complained that Humanist poetry was ridiculed and that the works of Cicero and Virgil were regarded with disdain. Instead he had to learn "misleading sophistries by tortuous syllogism and all the other lumber of contentious dialectic."[2] In spite of these resentments he worked hard enough to be awarded the baccalaureate in December, 1479.

In the meantime he had latinized his name, after the manner of other Humanists, from Konrad Bickel to Conradus Celtis (Bickel or Pickel = chisel = *caelum*) to which he added later the middle name Protucius (Greek: τυκοζ = chisel). After Heidelberg, where, as we have seen, he was introduced to classical studies by Agricola, he went to Erfurt, a fairly progressive university, which since the 1460s had harbored a steady stream of wandering Humanists such as Peter Luder, Jakob Publicius, and Samuel Karoch. Mutianus Rufus, the future head of the Erfurt Humanists, was his student here. Rostock and Leipzig seem to have been the next stations of Celtis's restless wanderings. In Leipzig he published a short work, his first, called *Ars versificandi et carminum* [The art of versifying and of poems]. Much more important than the technical instructions for the writing of poetry contained in this book was the philosophy behind it, most clearly expressed in the "Ode to Apollo" in the form of a prayer, which concludes the work.[3] Apollo, the inventor of poetry, is asked to leave his Greek home and come to the Germans, rough warriors and farmers though they may be, and teach them the fine art of composing poems.

Celtis dedicated his *Ars versificandi* to Frederick the Wise of Saxony—a prudent move, as it turned out, for the Elector was a good friend of Emperor Frederick III who had the power of crowning poet laureates. Not altogether surprisingly the young poet received this honor at the Diet of Nuremberg in 1487, though it is difficult to see in what way he had distinguished himself at that point except through the versifying manual and a few occasional poems. During the ceremony the emperor kissed the poet on his cheeks and invested him with all the privileges, honors, and liberties this title entailed. Throughout his life Celtis was very proud, perhaps inordinately so, of this title: he had a woodcut made by the famous Hans Burgkmair of himself as poet laureate and even introduced, for private use, his own chronology, occasionally dating letters after the year of his receipt of the laurel. There was, of course, a certain justification in his pride. Since Charles IV had first placed a laurel wreath on Petrarch's head some 140 years earlier, many distinguished, and a good number of less distinguished, poets had received this honor, all of them Italians. Celtis was the first German to get this recognition.

His colleagues in Leipzig were little impressed by the freshly crowned poet. A quarrel with some of his fellow professors prompted him to leave that city. Though this dispute was apparently of a purely personal nature and unrelated to any attacks on the *studia humanitatis,* it did not prevent the Humanists from magnifying it into the great controversy between Scholasticism and Humanism.

His departure or "expulsion," as the Humanists preferred to call it, from Leipzig provided Celtis with an opportunity to realize the dream of every German Humanist, to visit Italy, the cradle of the new movement. At age twenty-eight, in the summer of 1487, Celtis therefore crossed the Alps for the first and last time. Venice, Padua, Ferrara, Bologna, Florence, and Rome marked the stations of his Italian journey. Wherever he went he made contacts with Italian Humanists. In Ferrara, for instance, he met Battista Guarino, who had formerly been Agricola's teacher; in Florence he came to know Marsilio Ficino, well-known for his Platonic studies; and in Rome he joined the "Platonic Academy" of Pomponius Laetus, an organization founded with the aim of actively cultivating Humanist studies. It was here that Celtis first conceived the idea of founding similar societies in Germany, a plan he pursued with tireless energy after his return to his home country. On the whole, however, his stay in Italy proved to be a disappointment for him, strengthening his resentments rather than broadening his outlook. The disappointment was the result of a combination of petty frustrations and the inflated expectations of a Humanist who saw the discrepancy between the image he had of Roman civilization and the reality he found. Celtis, for example, took offense at having to kiss the Pope's feet, for in Germany it had been the emperor who had kissed his cheek. Similarly, he resented the snide remarks of some Italians about the alleged inferiority of German culture. But the greatest disappointment was Rome itself. What once had been the center of a universal culture had degenerated into a loud, profligate city torn by civil strife, corruption, and anarchy. Seeing Rome's ruins he wrote:

> What, oh Rome, is left, but the fame of your ruins of old times?
> Pride of the world were you once; consuls and Caesar walked here.
> Gluttonous Time in this world swallows up all things with a relish.
> Nothing exists that will last: virtue and books but remain.[4]

Following his studies in Cologne, Celtis had shown an intense interest in the natural sciences, in mathematics, and astronomy. Attracted by its excellent faculty in these fields, the German Humanist, after less than two years in Italy, left that country in the spring of 1489, for the University of Cracow in Poland where his teacher became the eminent scientist Albert Blarer of Brudzewo, a former student of Peuerbach and Regiomontanus and later the teacher of Copernicus. Of his experiences in Poland Celtis left us a vivid record in his later poems. We learn not only about a dangerous bison hunt or a frightening trip through the salt mines of Wieliczka but also about his passionate love affair with Hasilina of Rzytonic, the wife of a Polish nobleman. At the end of the summer of 1491 Celtis left Cracow and returned via Moravia and Bohemia to Nuremberg. A few months later, he moved to Ingolstadt at the invitation of his friend and benefactor Sixtus Tucher, hoping to find employment at the university. Though the anticipated resignation of his predecessor on the chair of poetry and rhetoric fell through, he did receive a temporary appointment in May, 1492. In a letter

to Tucher the Duke of Landshut-Bavaria, who was also the formal
head of the university, proposed forty or forty-two Rhenish gulden
as compensation. The treasurer naturally opted for the smaller
amount.[5]

In spite of the best intentions of the university's founders, Humanism led a Cinderella existence in Ingolstadt. Whether Celtis
was the most diplomatic man to make inroads into the predominance
of Scholasticism must be doubted, however, judging from the advertisement for his lectures that he was quick to post on the university bulletin board. In it, he deplored the poor Latin of some of
the professors who spoke, he maintained "like quacking geese or
lowing oxen disturbing the ears, pouring forth common, vile, and
corrupt words."[6] Such encomia were unlikely to endear him to his
new colleagues.

But these were the usual jibes exchanged between professors. Of
lasting importance was the inaugural lecture Celtis delivered in
August of the same year. Since it articulated some of the basic issues
of the intellectual debates of the time, it has been called a manifesto
of German Humanism. It was a passionate, brilliant speech which
one has to read in its entirety to get a feeling for the fervor and
engagement with which it was delivered. Intentionally without the
strict logical structure of a scholastic lecture, the speech resembles
a piece of music with a number of themes appearing, disappearing,
and contrasting each other.

What, then, are some of the themes discernible in that address?
Moral philosophy assumes for Celtis, as it had for Agricola, central
importance. Here too the precepts for leading a good and virtuous
life are to be found in the writings of ancient philosophers, poets,
and orators. But in contrast to the Frisian Humanist, whose speech
on philosophy, after all, had been delivered in Italy, Celtis injects
a national-patriotic element into his lecture, reminding his youthful
listeners, for example, that they do not bring credit but dishonor
to the German Empire if they neglect the study of letters in favor
of raising horses and dogs. Just as the Romans once took over from
the Greeks their empire and culture, so the Germans, who with the
Holy Roman Empire are already political heirs to Rome, are exhorted
to assume the cultural leadership in Europe, wresting it away from
the Italians. While six years earlier Celtis had prayed to Apollo to
bring the muses to Germany, he now aggressively summoned the
German youth to take the initiative.

Celtis's affiliation with Ingolstadt, lasting another five years until his call to Vienna in 1497, did not prevent him from engaging in a variety of other activities. In 1493, for example, he gave to the city council of Nuremberg his manuscript of the *Norimberga,* a masterful description of that city, and toward the end of the same year he made a sensational discovery in the monastery of St. Emmeran in Regensburg, a codex with the dramas of the tenth-century German nun Roswitha von Gandersheim, confirming his belief in the high culture of the Middle Ages. First circulating among his friends, the work was finally printed in 1501.

During that time the many-talented Celtis showed himself from yet another side—as organizer. His acquaintance with the academies of Ficino in Florence and Pomponius Laetus in Rome had convinced him of the value of such scholarly organizations. In Germany other considerations came into play. Whereas the Italian Humanists were generally regarded with sympathy because they presented themselves as the restorers of their own ancient civilization, the German Humanists were often viewed with considerable suspicion because of their teaching of non-Christian authors. The union of like-minded Humanists was therefore not only a matter of mutual encouragement but very often of survival in an indifferent, if not hostile, environment. For Celtis these groups became the concrete instruments for the realization of his cultural-patriotic goals.

The first of these associations was the "Academia Platonica" in Ingolstadt, a rather ambitious name for a small circle of Humanists assembled there. Much more important was his part in the founding of the "sodalitas Rhenana" in Heidelberg, where he had gone after the plague had temporarily closed the University of Ingolstadt. Johann von Dalberg, the good friend of the late Rudolf Agricola, was its president. Members included jurists, churchmen, scientists, and men of letters. Celtis must have enjoyed their companionship, for he stayed in Heidelberg long after Ingolstadt University had opened its doors again, so that the Count Palatinate, whose sons Celtis had been tutoring, was obliged to write a letter of excuse to the university. This delay was probably psychologically motivated. During his years in Ingolstadt Celtis had become increasingly disenchanted with that city, mocking its citizens as barbarous "turnip-eaters and beer-drinkers." He discharged his teaching obligations in a very casual manner, often dismissing classes on the flimsiest excuse. On one occasion, for example, he canceled his lecture because he claimed he had to sample a friend's new wine. Another time he went to the trouble of posting a poem on the university's bulletin board in which he vividly described attacks of fever and strong headaches. The students easily recognized them as the thinly disguised symptoms of a hangover. They wrote a bitter complaint to him, accusing him of calling them stupid, wild, and barbarous while he was living on their money. "Enough is enough," they declared, "you are rambling and disorganized: *clare docet qui clare intellegit*—he who thinks clearly also teaches clearly."[7]

Regrets on both sides were therefore minimal when Celtis, in March, 1497, accepted an invitation from the University of Vienna for a full-time lectureship in poetry and rhetoric, leaving the hated "turnip-eaters" and the Aristotle interpreters to their own devices.

With its almost eight hundred students, the University of Vienna was not only one of the largest but also one of the best-endowed institutions in Germany. Surprisingly early, since the middle of the fifteenth century, special lectures on ancient authors had been offered here. As in Heidelberg, Celtis became the initiator and organizer of a literary society, the so-called "Sodalitas litteraria Danubiana," a congregation that included Austrians, Germans, Bohemians, and Hungarians. From here the energetic Humanist also encouraged the establishment of similar groups in other German cities, envisioning a network of societies connected by common interests and friendships. In Strasbourg, Leipzig, Augsburg, Olmütz, Linz, and other cities such organizations sprang up. In Ingolstadt Jakob Locher, Celtis's student and successor, who had given himself the name Philomusus, founded one, calling it with his customary modesty "Philomusea sodalitas."[8] The self-imposed task of these sodalities was the editing and publication of classical authors, the mutual criticism and publication of their own works, the search for codices, and the collection of antiquities.

In Vienna Celtis enjoyed the special protection of Emperor Maximilian, who had captured the imagination of his age. Young, enthusiastic, and open-minded, he seemed to symbolize the aspirations of his time. Almost all Humanists lavishly praised him in whatever genre they thought they excelled. Celtis was no exception. For him, as for other Humanists, Maximilian was the restorer of the old imperial dignity and splendor. At Celtis's instigation, the emperor founded the College of Poets and Mathematicians. Although flourishing for a brief time and attracting such excellent students as Aventinus, Cuspinianus, Vadianus, Eck, and Zwingli, it disappeared after a number of years without apparent reason. During his years in Vienna Celtis also tried his hand at writing dramas. One of them, the *Ludus Dianae* [The play of Diana], is worth mentioning.[9] Performed on March 1, 1501, before the Emperor, his wife Bianca Maria Sforza, and the entire court in Linz, it has, in spite of its brevity (two hundred lines) the pretensions of a full-fledged classical play complete with a prologue and five acts. In each of the first three acts an ancient divinity pays homage to the Emperor (Diana, Silvanus, and Bacchus), while the fourth act takes a turn to the burlesque when Silvanus rides in on an obstinate donkey. The last act brings together all players in a hymn of thanks, with Diana speaking first and the chorus repeating the wish that Bianca, who by then had been married for seven years, may give birth to numerous children to fill the Austrian lands with archdukes. The ending was tactlessly out-of-place, of course, for Bianca's infertility had even been certified by medical experts and was well known at the court.

When Celtis, at the beginning of his poetic career, implored Apollo to descend from his Helicon and come to Germany, the Greek god responded graciously, and the poet he most inspired was none other than the Franconian Humanist himself. As a matter of fact, there is a surprising consensus among critics that Celtis is one of the best, if not the best, lyric poet of German Humanism.[10] All his poems are in Latin—a natural choice for Apollo perhaps, but not necessarily for a man so proudly patriotic as Celtis. However, for a Humanist, trained in Latin, there was no real alternative, since the German language at that time was incapable of expressing the shades of new ideas, in spite of the pioneering efforts of Wyle, Eyb, and Steinhöwel. The difference between Latin and German at that time becomes painfully obvious in comparisons of Latin works with the corresponding German translations. The polished hexameters of Virgil's *Aeneid,* for instance, were turned into clumsy doggerel verse by the Franciscan Thomas Murner.[11] It is therefore natural that the Humanists, who essentially wrote for each other, almost exclusively used the language of Cicero, Virgil, and Horace. This practice changed only with the Reformation when it was a matter of mobilizing public opinion for religious causes.

Celtis's major poetic work, and the only one that was published during his lifetime, was his *Quattuor Libri Amorum* [Four books of love poems]. In his long dedicatory letter to Maximilian, the poet felt obliged to defend these poems against possible charges of obscenity, claiming that they lead, by negative and positive example, to the recognition of true, and avoidance of false, love. As authorities Celtis cited the nun Roswitha von Gandersheim and the Holy Bible, two unimpeachable sources.[12] Yet the *Amores* were meant and indeed are much more than a collection of love poems. They are also a description of Germany from a geographical point of view. These two aspects, the erotic and geographical, are combined in such a way that each of the four love affairs takes place in a different part of Germany. But Celtis's fascination with numbers goes even further. Since there are nine muses, each of the four books is associated with nine different phenomena, which in turn occur in fours: the four seasons, the four ages of man, the four times of the day, the four cardinal points, the four temperaments, the four signs of the zodiac, the four temperatures, and the four basic colors. For all their clever schematic organization, the descriptions of the love adventures, half real, half fictitious, make delightful reading.

The first book tells of the poet's passionate love for the beautiful Polish woman Hasilina in Cracow (the East), an affair which is also documented through other sources. Among these is a still-existing letter written in Czech in which the lady complains about Celtis's indiscretion of circulating poems about their liaison.[13] Since Hasilina could not understand German or Latin and Celtis had no knowledge of Polish or Czech, the presence of a multilingual friend was required, at least initially. Unfortunately, the German Humanist was not Hasilina's only lover. At one point he had to wait outside in the cold while a priest received favors from her. After this rejection, which offered Celtis an opportunity to pour all his rage on the clergy, the poet was determined to renounce love and to dedicate his life entirely to the pursuit of knowledge. But while he is still thinking about these noble intentions, Cupid's arrows strike again: he falls in love with Elsula from Regensburg (the South), the heroine of the second book.

The third book finds the poet in Mainz, in the West, with Ursula. He bribes her with gifts. But hardly has she yielded to his entreaties when a jealous rival appears, forcing him to jump naked out of the window. He sprains his foot and, accompanied by the loud laughter of the stars, disappears limping into the night. The Ursula story, however, has a sad ending: his mistress dies of the plague. Nevertheless the pain over her loss does not prevent the poet from discussing the disastrous consequences of that epidemic disease in great detail.

In the fourth book the poet has aged: his hair has fallen out and his teeth have decayed. Nor is Barbara from Lübeck in the North, the heroine of that part, the youngest either. Moreover, she drinks a lot and likes to scold the poet, especially when she catches him in the arms of her maidservant.

Though accounts of trips to legendary Thule and Lapland found in the book are pure invention, Celtis did in fact draw on his many adventures experienced during the numerous hikes undertaken through all parts of Germany. These had made him a keen observer of the countryside, the people, and their customs. He therefore does not describe fictitious nymphs and shepherds, but concrete human beings. Moreover, he portrays them with unabashed sensuality, as in this poem called "Night and Hasilina's Kiss":

> How happy was I in that joyous hour,
> when kisses we exchanged time after time,
> and I was stroking Hasilina's breast so tenderly,
> now burying myself in her sweet lap,
> embracing now with delicate arms her body;
> fatigued by love I only then could sigh.
> How she kindled my fire with her own,
> forcing me to enlace my limbs with hers.
> Our souls did mingle in our mouths
> and that goddess, risen from the blue sea,
> tied us together with an adamantine chain.[14]

Against the Christian, spiritual ethics Celtis sets the eroticism of ancient Greek and Latin culture. Not concerns for the salvation of the soul but earthly, sensual love is in the center. The realism and intensity of the erotic descriptions combined with the perfection of the verses give his poems a position unsurpassed until the love poetry of the Baroque.

Although the *Amores* was the only collection of poems that appeared in print during Celtis's lifetime, it was not the only one that he composed. Five years after his death, in 1513, two of his former students edited and published *Libri Odarum Quattuor cum Epodo et Saeculari Carmine* [Four books of odes with an epode and the secular hymn]. The inclusion of the epode and the secular hymn point to the fact that this collection was patterned after that of Horace whose successor in Germany Celtis considered himself.

The *Odes* follow the same principle of organization as the *Amores:* each of the four books is devoted to a German region. Although they include poems about love, these recede into the background in favor of verses on Humanist friends. As a matter of fact, Celtis's itinerary in these four books is largely determined by the residences of his colleagues. These latter odes also provide us with interesting glimpses into the self-image of the German Humanists, who as a social group liked to set themselves off against the aristocracy on the one hand and their academic adversaries on the other. Conscious of their elitist status, they also disdained the common people, which in Celtis's case was ironic since he was of peasant stock himself.

Celtis was even less fortunate with the publication of his *Epigrams* which were not printed until more than 370 years after his death. This long lapse is all the more surprising as the author apparently had firmly intended to have the collection published as early as 1501/1502.[15] A bewildering variety of topics is covered in these five books of epigrams. Satirical poems on foes and detractors alternate with flattering verses on fellow Humanists and nobles; lines addressed to Saints Catherine and Anna are found next to those dedicated to the less saintly Hasilina; the seven world wonders are extolled, and so are the nine muses. There are also a number of epigrams which originally functioned as inscriptions, dedications, or epitaphs. Models for all these are Persius, Juvenal, and Martial.

The curious interweaving of amatory adventures and geographical descriptions in the *Amores* has pointed to one of the main themes of Celtis's oeuvre: his patriotic Humanism. It is not without significance that he used the forum of this collection to announce his intention of writing the *Germania illustrata,* that great project which was intended to combine geographical, historical, and ethnographic perspectives.[16] Through this horizontal (geographical) and vertical (historical) description of his native country, he hoped to achieve two goals: to make the Germans aware of their own cultural identity and to correct the view held by many foreigners, especially Italians, of Germany as a barbaric country. Although he had articulated these ambitious objects before in his Ingolstadt speech, it was in this work that he planned to realize them. Regrettably, the *Germania illustrata* was never written. However, a number of other works can be regarded as sketches for this patriotic enterprise. In addition to the multi-faceted *Amores,* Celtis published the *Germania generalis* [General description of Germany], which, in spite of its pretentious title, comprised only seven poems with a total of about two hundred lines.[17] Meant as a sort of down payment for the larger *Germania illustrata,* it starts out ambitiously with an account of the creation of the world, moves briskly to a description of Germany's four regions, dwells for a while on the Hercynian Forest, and then concludes, innocently enough, with verses on the quality of the German soil, a topic on which the wine-grower's son could speak with some authority.

The most convincing of these preliminary works, however, is his book on Nuremberg, the *Norimberga,* which he presented in manuscript to the council of that city in 1493.[18] Evidently disappointed by the small reward of a mere eight florins for his labors, he requested its return for "revisions." Only a decade later did he present it again to the authorities, now in printed form. In the meantime the thrifty city-fathers has increased the award to twenty Rhenish gulden. Today both sums seem pitifully inadequate, for in its genre the *Norimberga* is a masterpiece. Written in lively Latin prose, it is a portrait of the topography, architecture, customs, religious and cultural life, economic situation, and civic government of that important Franconian city.

Having contracted syphilis, apparently resulting from his amatory exploits, the German "arch-Humanist" died on February 4, 1508, not yet fifty years old. He was interred in St. Stephan's Cathedral in Vienna.

Because of his early death, Celtis did not see the fruits his labors bore in Germany. His poetry, his cultural nationalism, as well as his work for the establishment of literary societies all had an incalculable impact on future generations. Later poets, for instance, such as Eobanus Hessus, Euricius Cordus, and Petrus Lotichius gratefully acknowledged the debt to him as their master. Equally important was the profound effect he had on such men as Aventinus and Ulrich von Hutten through his patriotic writings. Lastly, though many of the Humanist organizations he inspired were of short duration, his ideas of a union of all German Humanists lived on, creating a sense of belonging together which was strengthened and reconfirmed through the controversy between the Cologne Dominicans and Johannes Reuchlin.

Johannes Reuchlin

Johannes Reuchlin was a lawyer by training and profession, yet he became famous throughout Europe as a Greek and Hebrew philologist. His first love was teaching; but only two years before his death, at age sixty-five, was he offered a professorship at a German university. His studies in ancient Hebrew were undertaken to arrive at a clearer understanding of the Holy Scriptures and theology, but it was precisely the theological faculty of the University of Cologne that attacked him so mercilessly. And finally, the quietness and peace of his study were all he desired in life, in this respect resembling Jakob Wimpfeling. And yet, unwillingly, he became the storm center of one of the most heated controversies of that time. These are some of the paradoxes that characterize the life of that great German Humanist.[19]

Born in the city of Pforzheim in 1455, Reuchlin enrolled at the age of fifteen at the University of Freiburg. Three years later, having entered the service of the Margrave of Baden-Durlach, he found himself appointed tutor to one of the latter's sons, with whom he went to Paris, the center of intellectual life in Europe throughout the Middle Ages and still a powerful magnet for students from many countries during the Renaissance. Here he met Johannes Heynlein von Stein, a fellow German from the village of Stein near Pforzheim, who was one of those not so rare individuals of that age who, though thoroughly anchored in Scholasticism, were also interested in that aspect of Humanism that helped to improve the knowledge of Latin through the reading of ancient authors. Active in many fields, he enjoyed a high reputation in Paris, where he was credited with having introduced printing with three fellow countrymen. Following Heynlin to Basel, Reuchlin attained his bachelor's and master's degree in 1475 and 1477. For lack of university instructors in Greek, the young scholar took private lessons from a certain Andronikus Contablakas. He also made the acquaintance of Sebastian Brant and through him met the eminent printer Johann Amerbach, who asked Reuchlin to compile a Latin dictionary, a task the impecunious student was more than willing to undertake. The Latin-Latin dictionary called *Vocabularius breviloquus* [Short dictionary] became very popular during that time being reprinted twenty-five times up to 1504, although *breviloquus* ("brief-speaking") is a rather infelicitous expression for that bulky five-hundred-page tome.

In 1478 Reuchlin returned to France where he continued his legal studies, first in Orleans and later in Poitiers, completing them with his licentiate diploma in 1481. At the invitation of Eberhard im Barte (1450–1496) he came to Tübingen a year later. As the reigning Count, later Duke of Württemberg, this son of Countess Palatine Mechthild was loved and respected by his people as a wise and peaceful man with a sense of justice. Though no scholar himself, he encouraged scholarship and had various ancient authors translated into German. Serving that ruler in several capacities, Reuchlin was to spend the next fourteen years at his court.

One of his first tasks was to accompany Eberhard as an interpreter on a journey to Rome, a trip that also included a brief stay in Florence, where the court of the Medici had become a center of Renaissance culture. Here Lorenzo de Medici, the family patriarch, had assembled not only an impressive circle of scholars and artists but also an extraordinary library, which deeply impressed the bookish scholar from Pforzheim. Reuchlin's flattering comments about it were answered by Lorenzo with a Latin pun. "My greatest treasures," he said, "are not my books [*libri*] but my children [*liberi*]."[20] Little did he know, of course, that one of these children was the future Pope Leo X. Twenty-five years later Reuchlin reminded that Pope of his visit to the magnificent city on the Arno, saying "Florentia illo aevo nihil erat floridius" ("at that time nothing was more flourishing than Florence"). As a pun, the compliment was not much better than Lorenzo's but it was, no doubt, meant just as sincerely.

After his return to Germany, Reuchlin moved to Stuttgart, the residence of Eberhard. As Assessor of the Supreme Court, Counselor, as well as practicing lawyer, he was to remain in this city, with some interruptions, for the rest of his life. Unlike Agricola and Celtis, who preferred to remain bachelors, Reuchlin married. But it sheds an interesting light on the position of women at that time that neither the name of his first nor that of his second wife is known, although otherwise minute details of his life have been preserved for us through his extensive correspondence.

A second trip to Italy, again undertaken on behalf of Eberhard, allowed him to make contacts with several important scholars, among them Pico della Mirandola and Hermolaus Barbarus. The latter, a well-known Venetian scholar and philologist, became his Latin teacher and also called him "Capnion," Greek for Reuchlin ("little smoke"), a name he used only rarely, and then jokingly, in his correspondence with Italian Humanists. His meeting with Mirandola, however, was to have far-reaching consequences because the Italian philosopher had tried to find a common ground between Greek philosophy, the Jewish cabala, and Christian theology. Attempting a similar synthesis, Reuchlin became, to a certain extent, Pico's successor.

Through his diplomatic work for Eberhard, the Swabian Humanist also made the acquaintance of the old Emperor Frederick III, who was so much impressed by his skills that he elevated Reuchlin to the rank of nobility. He not only gave him a coat of arms but also made him a Count Palatine and allowed him to confer doctoral degrees. Although Reuchlin occasionally used the coat of arms—an altar with coals from which smoke (Reuchlin) rose—he never made use of the other privileges granted to him. While at the court in Linz, he also began to study ancient Hebrew under the emperor's Jewish doctor, Jacob ben Jehiel Loans.

The death of Eberhard im Barte in 1496 proved to be a turning point in Reuchlin's life. Under the duke's reckless and irresponsible successor, Eberhard the Younger, an Augustinian monk called Conrad Holzinger, an old enemy of Reuchlin, was released from jail and given substantial powers. Fearing for his life, the Humanist left Stuttgart and accepted an invitation extended by Johann von Dalberg, the Bishop of Worms and chancellor of the Elector of the Palatinate, to come to Heidelberg. Though Reuchlin would have liked to give public lectures on Greek and Hebrew, he was apparently prevented from doing so by monks friendly to Holzinger. Instead he was appointed to the position of counselor and supreme educator (*oberster Zuchtmeister*) of the Elector's two sons for an annual salary of one hundred florins, two horses, and a courtly suit of clothes. Another diplomatic mission to Rome (1495) gave him the opportunity to widen his intellectual horizons. This time he continued his Hebrew studies, taking lessons from the excellent Jewish scholar Obadje Sforno.

In the meantime, Eberhard the Younger had been deposed and a caretaker government formed. Much to the regret of his Heidelberg friends, Reuchlin therefore returned to Stuttgart where he stayed until political unrest again forced him to leave that city. He greatly deplored having to leave behind the greater part of his library or, as he called it, "The other half of my soul" (*dimidium animae*). At age sixty-five, the man who had done so much for Greek and Hebrew studies in Germany, was appointed professor in Ingolstadt, a position he held only briefly, for in 1521 he returned to Stuttgart, where he died the following year.

During his stay in Heidelberg Reuchlin wrote two Latin comedies, *Scenica progymnasmata* or *Henno* and *Sergius*.[21] The latter's subtitle, *Caput capitis* [The head of the head] gives a clue to the contents of this short, witty, but not theatrically effective play in which a head, or rather, a skull, is the protagonist. The opening scene shows us some friends who are accompanied by a stranger, called Buttabatta, who carries something under his coat. Only after repeated entreaties by his curious companions is he willing to reveal his secret: it is a dirty, evil-smelling skull. Jokingly the friends recommend to him to pretend it is the head of a saint but advise him to subject it to a thorough cleaning first. Having done this, the stranger reappears with the sparklingly clean skull, praising eloquently its wonderful ability to do what you want it to do—for instance, to promote, demote, raise from the dead, and make rich or poor. The friends kiss the skull like the relic of a saint. When they insist, however, on knowing whose head it was, Buttabatta declares that it once belonged to Sergius, an impudent beggar who, during his lifetime, had been expelled from a monastery because of immoral conduct. Converted to Islam, Sergius is said to have persecuted his former fellow Christians with utmost cruelty. Frightened, the friends now curse the skull and its bearer.

The play gave Reuchlin an opportunity to indulge in a small literary vendetta against his enemy Holzinger, who after his release from prison had become the "head of the head," that is, the principal advisor of Eberhard the Younger. But the play is more than a personal attack on an old foe. It also satirizes the monks in general and ridicules the worship of relics in particular. It is understandable that twenty years later this comedy became a favorite with the Reformers who shared the Humanist's aversion to monks and relics. But it is also easy to see why the cautious Dalberg advised against a public performance of this play, for fear that it might offend influential Franciscans at the Heidelberg court.

Reuchlin's friends in that city, however, encouraged him to write another, less controversial play, the performance of which was less likely to be subjected to the benevolent veto of his old friend Dalberg. The title *Scenica progymnasmata* [Training through theater] points to the pedagogical nature of the plot.[22] It was meant to train students in the use of Latin, especially that of Plautus and Terence. Divided into five acts separated by choral passages it followed the style of ancient comedy.

The farmer Henno steals eight golden pieces from his wife Elsa and sends his servant Dromo to the cloth merchant Danista to fetch some cloth for a new jacket. Instead of following these instructions, Dromo buys the cloth on credit, immediately sells it, and pockets the profit as well as the original eight gold pieces. In the meantime, Elsa has discovered the theft. At the suggestion of a neighbor she consults the astrologer Albucicius who gives her a description of the thief which fits her husband exactly. The cheated cloth merchant now sues Dromo. But during the trial, the latter, on the advice of his devious lawyer Petrucius, pretends to be feeble-minded and answers all questions posed by the judge with a sheepish "ble." Naturally, he is acquitted. However, when the lawyer wants his fee, Dromo continues to answer all questions and requests with a monotonous "ble." The fee is, of course, never paid. The play, however, ends on a happy note. Dromo, restored to a more conventional speech after the lawyer's departure, marries the farmer's daughter, and receives the stolen money as a dowry.

With this comedy Reuchlin surpassed the few Latin Humanist comedies that had been written before him in Germany. The action is quick, the satire on the dishonest astrologer and greedy lawyer biting, and the language clear and to the point. In writing this play, the German Humanist used some motifs of the well-known French farce *Maître Pathelin,* although the basic structure of the plot as well as the various character types seem to have come from Italy.[23]

The work was enormously successful. Between 1498 and 1523 it was printed thirty-one times. But only in 1531 did a German adaptation appear: Hans Sachs's *Henno,* a name that is now also used for Reuchlin's Latin version instead of the more cumbersome Latin title. The contemporary German Humanists reacted predictably. Brant wrote a prologue for the printed edition, claiming that under his friend's leadership the old comedy had revisited Germany. Celtis did what he always used to do on such occasions, he wrote an ode. And Wimpfeling recommended the reading in his *Isidoneus,* comparing Reuchlin to Plautus and Terence, an ever so slight exaggeration.

The publication and success of these two comedies are all the more remarkable as Reuchlin was a serious scholar, the first German who was truly trilingual, i.e., competent in the three classical languages, Latin, Greek, and Hebrew. That he was thoroughly familiar with the Latin language and its literature was not particularly remarkable in an age in which this was the universal language. More unusual, however, was his proficiency in Greek. When a Greek scholar in Italy once heard Reuchlin read and translate Thucydides, he is said to have exclaimed, "From our exile Greece has flown across the Alps."[24] Such praise for the young man—Reuchlin was twenty-seven years old—might seem a little extravagant, but the truth is that the German Humanist considered himself the first propagator of Greek in Germany—a claim that is fully justified. Through his example, his oral teachings, and his insistence on the study of Greek, Reuchlin contributed to the introduction of that language into the curriculum at a time when very few educated Germans knew Greek.

Remarkable as Reuchlin's achievements in Latin and Greek may have been, they pale in comparison to his pioneering studies in ancient Hebrew. With his work *De rudimentis Hebraicis* [The fundamentals of Hebrew, 1506], the first Hebrew grammar and dictionary written by a Christian scholar, he laid the basis for the European study of Hebrew.[25] In the introduction to this work Reuchlin details the reasons that have prompted him to undertake such a task. In his opinion a knowledge of Hebrew was essential for an understanding of the foundations of the Christian teachings, especially the Bible. However, since Jews have been expelled from many countries, there is the real danger that familiarity with their tongue may disappear. He therefore considers it his duty to preserve the sacred language. Fully aware of his historic accomplishment, Reuchlin concludes the preface with a famous line from Horace: "Exegi monumentum aere perennius" ("I raised a monument more lasting than bronze"). His pride was fully justified. With this work, he made possible a broad study of Hebrew language and literature by Christian scholars and thus paved the way to a philological understanding of the Bible.

Unlike his successful Latin dictionary, however, this pioneering Hebrew grammar was a commercial failure—a consolation to all modern scholars in a similar situation. Out of the 1000 copies printed only 250 were sold.

Reuchlin was a devout Christian and, as mentioned, his studies in ancient Hebrew were meant to strengthen Christian thought. This is also true of his inquiries into the cabala, an esoteric body of Jewish mystical tradition, literature, and thought which Leo

Rosten has described in the following way: "Cabalism was a movement of profound mystical faith fused to, and steeped in, the su-
perstitions and occult preoccupations of the pre-Middle Ages. It
was a minor but meaningful stream of thought and experience, a
pious attempt to fathom the awesome, fearful mysteries of God and
creation. Originally, cabalism meant Oral Tradition; in the twelfth
century, Jewish mystics adopted the term, claiming an unbroken
link between their ideas and those of ancient days."[26] For the ca-
balist, letters were only signs of things. This not only meant that
scriptures had to be deciphered according to the sense of each word,
but that all of nature was a system of correspondences reflecting the
divine creation. Since one of the fundamental theses of the cabala
was the notion of a strict parallelism between the visible and invisible
world, a knowledge of the proper techniques of interpretation was
of paramount importance for unlocking the secrets that lay beneath
the surface of the literal sense.

The first time a portion of the cabala appeared in writing was in
the thirteenth century when Mosche de Leon recorded the Book of
Zohar *(Splendor)*. Since it was written in an artificial form of Aramaic,
it was understood only by a small circle of scholars. It was the great
Italian Humanist Pico della Mirandola who really made the Christian
world aware of the works of that mystical movement. Although his
attempts to harmonize Greek philosophy, Jewish cabala, and Christian theology into one great synthesis initially met with considerable
skepticism on the part of the Church so that he was obliged to
defend himself in a trial, he was eventually acquitted of all charges
by Pope Alexander VI. It is highly probable that Pico inspired
Reuchlin to study the cabala. Both men had met, as we recall,
during the latter's second journey to Italy.

The first fruit of Reuchlin's cabalistic studies was his work *De
verbo mirifico* [On the wonder-working word, 1494]. It is written
in the form of a dialogue between the Greek philosopher Sidonius,
the Jew Baruchias, and Reuchlin himself. Although each participant
dominates the scene on one of the three days of the debate, the
Christian Reuchlin has the final word. A bewildering variety of
topics is discussed, such as faith, miracles, the power of words and
figures, secret rules, and the mysteries of the seals.

Reuchlin's *De arte cabalistica* [On the cabalistic art], published
twenty-three years later, was a much more mature work. In the
meantime, he had been deeply absorbed in Hebrew literature, be-

coming, in fact, the leading Christian scholar of Hebrew in Europe and gaining international prominence through his controversy with the theologians of Cologne. When he finished the book, the trial against him was still pending before a court of the Roman Curia. His dedication of the work to Pope Leo X must therefore be viewed as a not-so-subtle attempt to influence his Holiness.

Like his first work, *De arte cabalistica* is written in the form of a conversation, this time between the Jew Simon, the Muslim Marranus, and the Greek Philolaus, who happen to meet in Frankfurt. While in the first and third books Simon has the floor, explaining and praising the teachings of the cabala, Philolaus elucidates the ideas of Pythagoras in the second, trying to prove their identity with those of the cabala. Both cabalists and Pythagoreans, he argues, assume the existence of two worlds and believe in a messiah. Pythagoreans further hold that faith is a product of divine revelation and that all creatures are emanations of God's mind. The messiah is considered as the redeemer of mankind, and salvation consists in a constant waiting for God. Pythagorean philosophy possesses, like the cabala, a secret knowledge of numbers. It is this intricate numerology and the insistence to go beyond the literal sense of the word and find its hidden meaning that may constitute the most obvious resemblance between the cabala and Greek philosophy as it is represented here by Pythagoreanism.

The impact of Reuchlin's two cabalistic works was considerable. Though Erasmus, who was too much of a rationalist to be touched by this esoteric mysticism, confessed that the cabala, the Talmud, and Pythagorean philosophy "had never smiled at him," other thinkers like Karlstadt and Paracelsus and, above all, Agrippa von Nettesheim (1486–1535) were profoundly influenced by Reuchlin.[27] One hundred years after the latter's death, a scholar inadvertently referred to Reuchlin as "Rabbi Capnion." A modern critic, commenting on this error, has declared: "In sober truth, this epithet was well deserved, for his services to the cause of Hebrew literature were far greater than were those of many an officially consecrated rabbi."[28]

It is one of the ironies of Reuchlin's life that this erudite and quiet scholar was to become the center of the most polemical controversy prior to the Reformation. Never before, not even in the acrimonious Locher-Wimpfeling feud, had the conflict between the Humanists and the conservative theologians been brought out in such sharpness and with so much fervor as in this dispute, which dragged on for over a decade.[29]

It all started when Johann Pfefferkorn, a Jew who had converted to Christianity, wrote four books (*Judenspiegel* [Mirror of Jews, 1507]; *Judenbeichte* [The Jews' confession, 1508]; *Osternbuch* [Book of Easter, 1509], and *Judenfeind* [The Jews' enemy, 1509]) denouncing the Jews for their allegedly usurious practices and hatred of Christians, and demanding, among other things, the confiscation of their books. In August, 1509, Pfefferkorn succeeded in obtaining a mandate from Emperor Maximilian authorizing him to collect all Jewish books with the assistance of the local authorities and a parish priest and to destroy those that called into question Christian tenets and upheld Judaism. As Pfefferkorn proceeded to realize his plan with a convert's zeal, a number of influential Jews complained to the emperor, who thereupon directed the Archbishop of Mainz to seek expert opinions in this matter from the universities of Mainz, Cologne, Erfurt, and Heidelberg, as well as from individual scholars. Cologne University responded quickly in favor of Pfefferkorn. Erfurt and Mainz followed suit, while Heidelberg equivocated. Jakob Hochstraten, the Dominican Inquisitor General in Cologne, not surprisingly, concurred with his colleagues from the university.

There was, however, one man who spoke out clearly and boldly against the measures proposed by Pfefferkorn. That man was Johannes Reuchlin. Though couched in the dispassionate language of a legal brief, his *Gutachten* [Legal opinion] is an eloquent plea for tolerance and understanding at a time of religious bigotry, narrow-mindedness, and intolerance.[30]

Adhering closely to the question whether there are any legal grounds for confiscating and destroying the books of the Jews, Reuchlin divides Hebrew literature into seven classes, examining each in turn as to its potential harm to Christianity. Since Christians have incorporated the Old Testament (1) into their own canon, there is obviously no reason for banning it. Similarly, there are no grounds for excluding the Talmud (2), that massive and monumental compendium of debates, dialogues, and commentaries on the Torah, because it contains nothing that is contrary to Christian doctrine. The same is true for the cabala (3), Jewish glosses and commentaries (4), speeches, disputations, and collections (5), and the works of Jewish philosophers and scholars of all disciplines (6). Only in the last division, which comprises fables, poems, fairy tales, satires, and collections of poems, does Reuchlin find some works, though very few, that slander the Christian God, Jesus, and the Holy Virgin. Yet he is quick to add that these writings have, in most cases, been destroyed by the Jews themselves. However, if any of these ostensibly slanderous works are found, the Humanist scholar suggests, they should be confiscated but not burnt, "for the Jews have written these books in their interest for the protection of their faith, whenever they were attacked by someone, whether he was heathen, Turk, or Christian."³¹ No Christian has therefore the right to make any decision about Jews, nor should the latter be called heretics since heretic is a name for those who renounce the Christian faith.

Yet for these noble sentiments, the Hebrew scholar was no Gotthold Ephraim Lessing, who demonstrated the essential equality of Islam, Judaism, and Christianity, three hundred years later, in his drama *Nathan der Weise* [Nathan the Wise]. For Reuchlin, however, Christianity was the only true path to God, and every Christian's duty was the conversion of "unbelievers." But unlike Pfefferkorn, who advocated coercion and violence, he argued for friendliness, gentleness, and persuasion. There should be a dialogue between the two religions, he maintained, and to be better equipped for this dialogue, Christians should study the works of the Jews.

After receiving these conflicting opinions, the Emperor decided that he needed more time for study. Nothing happened to the Jewish books neither then nor later, and those that had been confiscated were returned. With that the matter could have rested, for what happened in the following years had little to do with the initial incident, the confiscation of Hebrew books.

Pfefferkorn's reaction to Reuchlin's *Gutachten* was a passionate pamphlet called the *Handspiegel* [Hand mirror, 1511], in which he accused his opponent of corruption and plagiarism, a charge that deeply hurt Reuchlin as a scholar and man of integrity. Stung to the quick, he immediately issued the *Augenspiegel* [Eye mirror, 1511]. Carried away by his rage, Reuchlin not only sank to the polemical level of his attacker but also retreated considerably—and for our modern taste too much—from his unconditional defense of the Talmudic books. At the same time he inveighed against the theological faculty of Cologne, which was backing Pfefferkorn. Consequently, one of their representatives, Arnold von Tungern, published a pamphlet in which he called some of the articles and propositions in the *Augenspiegel* heretical. Moreover, the Cologne theologians succeeded in obtaining an imperial order prohibiting the sale of Reuchlin's book.

The debate was further heated up by Pfefferkorn's *Brandspiegel* [Fire mirror, 1512] in which he vehemently denounced his former fellow believers, suggesting their expulsion from Worms, Frankfurt, and Regensburg and the taking away of their children. The Jews, he claimed, are favored by Reuchlin. The latter answered with an equally slanderous work, his *Defensio,* in which he called his opponents sheep, swine, horses, mules, heathens, and devil's disciples. His special scorn was reserved for Ortvinus Gratius of the Cologne faculty whom he branded an ignoramus knowing neither Latin nor Greek.

The enraged theologians of Cologne retaliated by having Reuchlin's *Defensio* suppressed by imperial decree. In addition, they asked the theological faculties of Mainz, Louvain, and Erfurt for opinions on the *Augenspiegel* as well as requesting a judgment from their own university. Not surprisingly, all four condemned the work. To make the victory over Reuchlin complete, Jakob von Hochstraten cited the German Humanist before his court of inquisition in Mainz on a charge of heresy, acting both as prosecutor and judge. These outrageous proceedings, however, were stopped by the Archbishop of Mainz, and Reuchlin was given a chance to appeal to Pope Leo X. The Roman Curia referred the matter back to the Bishop of Speyer, who totally acquitted Reuchlin of any crimes. The *Augen-spiegel* was declared neither dangerous nor heretical. Hochstraten at once appealed to Rome.

That was in March, 1514. Powerful lobbies for and against the German Humanist formed. Emperor Maximilian threw his weight behind Reuchlin, while Charles I of Spain and Francis I of France exercised their influence in favor of Hochstraten and his followers. Torn between these political pressure groups, the Curia diplomatically postponed a decision so that the actual verdict was not pronounced until 1520, six years later. By that time, interest in the case had largely waned not only because of the length of the litigation but also because of the increasing absorption with the Reformation. Mistakenly identifying Luther's rebellion with the Humanist cause, Rome declared the *Augenspiegel* to be offensive, ordered its destruction, and saddled Reuchlin with the costs of the lengthy trial.

The Letters of Obscure Men

Six years before Rome's final judgment, however, Reuchlin published a collection of letters written to him over the years by well-known men from all over Europe. Most of these letters—*Clarorum virorum epistolae* [Letters of famous men]—had nothing to do with the controversy about the Hebrew books, and some correspondents, like Rudolf Agricola, had been dead long before the quarrel broke out. The object of the anthology was thus not so much to show support for the position Reuchlin had taken in this particular case but to underline the esteem he enjoyed by his scholarly peers such as Pico della Mirandola, Johann Geiler von Kaysersberg, Conrad Peutinger, Beaṭus Rhenanus, Willibald Pirckheimer, Joachim Vadianus, and Mutianus Rufus, to list only a few of the better-known names. This collection would be forgotten along with similar testimonials had it not provided the foil for one of the most famous books of that period and one of the main contributions of sixteenth-century German Humanism to world literature, the *Epistolae obscurorum virorum* [Letters of obscure men].[32]

Appearing anonymously in March, 1515, the *Epistolae obscurorum virorum* mentioned no editor, had no preface and no dedication, but listed as printer one Aldus Minutius while showing as the publication date "the above-mentioned year." Since no year was mentioned above, however, and the name of the famous Venetian printer suggested on the title page was spelled Manutius, the more perceptive readers must have realized that a game was being played with them. Some months later, a second edition appeared, expanded by seven letters, and in 1517 a completely new compilation with sixty-two different epistles came out. Obviously in keeping with the clever game they played with the public, the authors stated the Roman Curia as the place of publication, the unlikeliest place to come out with such a product, as we shall see.

What, then, in fact are the *Letters of Obscure Men?* They are nothing less than a fictitious correspondence presumably written by Scholastics among themselves but actually composed by certain Humanists who supported Reuchlin. In contrast to the real, famous men *(clari viri)* on Reuchlin's side, these alleged followers of the theologians of Cologne are called *obscuri,* that is, "unknown." The simple but brilliant device of presenting the counterfeit set of letters as real allows the authors, who will be discussed later, to make the obscure men reveal themselves before the reader's eyes.

Not unexpectedly, the obscure men are portrayed as staunchly orthodox Christians. Those suspected of thinking even slightly differently are termed heretics worthy of being burnt at the stake. In addition, the "spiritus sanctus" is constantly invoked and the letters are generously sprinkled with supporting quotations from Scripture. For all their piety, the obscure men purport to be no mean scholars however, and they employ their considerable intellectual powers in the solution of such "important" questions as whether one commits a mortal or venial sin when one eats an egg with a little chicken on Friday (Eov II 26). Similarly, the problem of whether Reuchlin's *Augenspiegel* should be burnt at the stake for being heretical or whether it should be hanged, like a thief, for stealing Pfefferkorn's honor is discussed in a tone of seriousness. The proposed solutions to these problems are supported by irrefutable quotations from the Bible, Aristotle, or Scholastic handbooks. Moreover, the syllogistic method is employed with the greatest acumen—and to the most trivial ends—so that occasionally a letter seems to run in circles as in the following example where a certain Guilhelmus Scherscleifferius writes to Gratius:

I am wondering very much, esteemed sir, why you do not write to me and yet write to others who write not as often to you as I write to you. If you are my enemy and do not want to write to me any longer, at least write to me why you do not write to me any longer so that I know why you do not write although I always write to you and though I know that you will not write back to me. (Eov I 15)

The preoccupation of the obscure men with such seemingly weighty problems, however, does not unduly interfere with their life of leisure and pleasure. Reports on feasting and drinking occupy a broad space in these letters. And so do the accounts of their amatory adventures. As a matter of fact, Conrad von Zwickau, the only *obscurus* who is given three letters, in contrast to the others, who have to be satisfied with one each, has nothing on his mind except love. If he needs any justification for his activities he finds it in a syllogism: "Amor is love, and God is love—therefore Amor is not a bad thing" (Eov I 13). Similarly, if two theologians should seek the favors of the same girl, the peaceful God-seekers suggest a time-sharing arrangement, as Arnold von Tungern does to Ortvin. However, being brought up in a hierarchical society, Tungern proposes to do this sharing according to rank: "I today and you tomorrow—the worthiest first: I the doctor, you the magister" (Eov I 45). It is significant that the only work by a classical author they allegedly know is Ovid's *Ars amatoria* [Art of love]. Otherwise these stalwart theologians are described as preferring to quote Saint Jerome's dictum "Poetria est cibus diaboli" ("poetry is the devil's food"), for poets, they maintain, are notorious liars and should therefore not be read. If the ancient poets are unknown, the modern poets, as which the Humanists were commonly referred to, suffer the same fate. Nowhere does this become clearer than in the letter of a certain Antonius who happens to meet Erasmus of Rotterdam, of whom he has never heard, in Strasbourg. But since everybody considers the famous Erasmus a learned man, Antonius wants to impress the master with his contention that he does not believe that Caesar wrote the *Commentaries*. His argument goes as follows, "Whoever is concerned with arms and is busy with work all the time, cannot learn Latin. But Caesar was always engaged in war and great works. Therefore he could not have become lettered and learned Latin. I therefore believe that no other than Suetonius wrote these commentaries, for I have never seen anybody who has a style more similar to Caesar than Suetonius" (Eov I 42). Here, in a few lines, we have a striking example of the techniques of self-revelation. First of all, Antonius's ignorance of Erasmus's stature as a European Humanist unmasks him as a man out of step with the times. Furthermore, his employment of the syllogistic method shows to what absurd ends this technique could be misused, and finally his insensitivity to the stylistic differences of two major Latin authors exposed him as a complete illiterate—at least in Humanist eyes.

In order to give unity and direction to their literary endeavors, the authors of the *Epistolae obscurorum virorum* decided to have all obscure men write to one person instead of making them address the letters to each other. The man whom they selected and who thus had the dubious distinction of becoming for all times the butt of the Humanists' scorn and derision was Ortvin Gratius. There were probably two reasons for choosing him as the recipient of these fictitious letters. First of all, he had been involved in the controversy from the beginning, when he translated Pfefferkorn's German pamphlets into Latin. Having also contributed his own Latin verses to

the convert's tracts, he was thus suspected to be the main force
behind the attacks on Reuchlin. But the Humanists especially de-
spised him for being a renegade, for he had been educated, like
many other Humanists, by Alexander Hegius in Deventer and was
therefore considered a Humanist of sorts himself.

If Ortvin was seen as a deserter from the cause in the eyes of
Humanists, he was considered the infallible master by the obscure
men. He alone was found capable of passing judgment, of giving
advice, and of hearing their complaints. He was regarded as the
source of all wisdom and the object of their solicitude. When Fi-
lipazzo of Antwerp, for instance, learned from a Dominican that
Ortvin was in ill health, he was so shocked, he tells us, that he
fainted in the middle of the street and could only be revived by a
cold shower and the tickling of his pubic hair (Eov I 41). Moreover,
that Ortvin's capacity for self-denial was not highly developed in
no way diminished his high standing with his friends. If anything,
it enhanced it. Sexual relations between Pfefferkorn's wife and Ortvin
are repeatedly alluded to. When Pfefferkorn gently drops a hint to
his friend, saying, "Sir, I wish you would eat from your own plate
and let me eat from mine" (Eov I 39), Ortvin pretends not to
understand.

One of the most amusing aspects of the *Epistolae* is the language.
To be sure, the work is in Latin, but it is an idiom that is a far cry
from the Ciceronian Latin the Humanists tried to imitate. Ulrich
von Hutten, the eminent German Humanist, expressed it succinctly
when he said "barbare ridentur barbari" ("the barbarians are being
laughed at in a barbarian way"). "Barbarian," however, in this
context means that the Latin is based largely on German syntax,
structure, and even, to some extent, vocabulary, explaining the
conversational and even chatty tone of these letters. "When the
vespers are over *(aus),*" for instance, is literally translated as "quando
vesperae sunt ex." *Cum* always means *mit* ("with"), so that *mitkommen*
("to come along") is translated as *cum ire*. Unaware of the nonex-
istence of a Latin indefinite article, the *obscuri* blithely render *ein*
and *eine* with *unus* and *una*. Their very names are either direct Latin
translations of German names, as in *Plumilegius* ("feather-picker"),
Caprimulgius ("goat milker") *Mellilambius* ("honey licker") and *Lig-
nipercussor* ("woodchopper") or German names with a Latin ending,
as in *Straussfederius* ("ostrich feather"), *Mistladerius* ("manure-loader"),
and *Buntschuhmacherius* ("shoemaker"). With the same innocence

they occasionally latinize German words by adding a Latin ending to the German term, as in *zecha, zechare* (German: *Zeche, zechen* = carouse), *landsmannus* (German: *Landsmann* = fellow countryman), *kaufmannus* (German: *Kaufmann* = merchant), and *landsknechtus* (German: *Landsknecht* = mercenary). Similarly the grammar is simplified. Instead of the involved syntax of classical Latin with its predilection for subordinate clauses, they prefer the stringing together of brief main clauses.

Who were the authors of this satire? Since it appeared anonymously, the doors for speculation were thrown wide open. Among the numerous contemporary writers given credit (or blame) for authoring the book were Erasmus and Reuchlin. Both firmly denied the charge. Only since the beginning of this century, thanks mainly to the research done by Walther Brecht and Aloys Bömer, can we be reasonably sure of the authors.[33] The researchers' findings can be summed up as follows. The idea of the *Epistolae* was probably hatched in the Erfurt Humanist circle. The main credit for the first part has to be given to Crotus Rubeanus who was responsible for the general concept and organization of the work. Next to him, Ulrich von Hutten contributed I 1 and the Humanist Hermann von dem Busche I 19, 36, 61, 62, and possibly 12 and 39. Hutten was also responsible for the appendix to the first part and the majority of letters of the second part. Only in II 13, 17, 29, 42, 61, and 62 is Hutten's authorship in doubt. For the first four of this group his friend Jakob Fuchs is claimed as an author.

Crotus Rubeanus, the remarkable author of the first part, was born Johannes Jäger (hunter) in Dornheim near Arnstadt in Thuringia. After Humanist fashion he latinized his name, first into Venator or Venatorius, later into the more esoteric Crotus, the mythical hunter who was transposed to the stars by Jupiter, then adding Rubeanus after his home town (Dornheim—thornhome; Latin: *rubus* = bramble bush). Beginning in 1498 he studied in Erfurt, where he was, for five years, the friend of Martin Luther. While the latter entered the monastery of the Augustinians in 1505, Crotus went to the monastery of Fulda, from which he probably helped his freedom-loving friend Ulrich von Hutten, who had been sent there by his parents, to escape. Going together to Cologne, a bastion of Scholasticism, both encountered there the methods of syllogistic deductions and disputations which they later so mercilessly satirized in the fictitious letters. No wonder that the two friends did not stay very long but returned to Erfurt, where Crotus soon joined the circle of young Humanists around Mutianus Rufus. Social disturbances, however, forced him to leave that city in 1509, and soon afterwards he became headmaster of the school in Fulda. He stayed here until 1516, acquiring firsthand knowledge of the monastic life, and there is no doubt that the monks of that abbey served him as prototypes for the obscure men. Meanwhile, Ulrich von Hutten, the principal author of the second part of the satire, whose life and works will be discussed later, after leaving his friend Crotus in Erfurt in 1506, set out on a vagrant life which took him to various German university towns and twice to Italy. While in Rome for the second time, he learned of the appearance in print of the *Epistolae* and started to work on the second part, which was published in 1517.

There are considerable thematic and stylistic differences between the two sections. While Crotus does not take the obscure men too seriously, and his humor remains good-natured and playful, we see in Hutten the future reformer's indignation about the abuses of the Church, the monks, and theologians. His tone is shriller, his wit more vindictive. Furthermore, although the Reuchlin affair plays only a marginal role in the first part, it moves into the center in the second where the successes and setbacks of the controversy are recounted in detail. Here we get a lively eyewitness account, though of course a fictitious and thus satirically distorted one, of the efforts and machinations of the Hochstraten lobby to obtain a positive verdict from the curial court. A certain brother Johann von Werdau, for instance, reports to Gratius from Rome:

I hope that I may soon be able to send you good news, for Herr Doctor Jakob von Hochstraten is doing his best. The other day he gave a banquet, inviting many old and experienced courtiers and an apostolic secretary who is in high favor with his Holiness and several members of the Rota. He entertained them with partridges, pheasants, hares, and fresh fish and the choicest Corsican and Greek wines. And all guests said, "He treated us with the greatest reverence. He is indeed a remarkable theologian. We will be on his side. (Eov II 5)

The Humanists were naturally delighted with this satire directed against their arch-enemies. The story was told that Erasmus, when reading a copy lent him by a friend, "fell into such a fit of laughter that an abscess on his face burst, which else should have been laid open by order of his physician."[34] There were other benefits besides the free treatment of an annoying abscess on the countenance of the great Dutch Humanist. The controversy, up to that time confined to a small circle of scholars, now became a matter of public concern. Pope Leo X contributed his share to publicizing the matter by issuing a bull in 1517 banning the book and admonishing the faithful to give up any copies they possessed. Furthermore, the authors were threatened with excommunication, an empty threat since the work had appeared anonymously. Finally, the clergy were ordered to denounce the work publicly from the pulpit, in the vernacular if necessary, giving it the best advertisement the Humanists could have hoped for.[35]

The battle lines were clearly drawn. On the one hand stood the progressive Humanists, on the other the backward-looking theologians and Scholastic philosophers. This division into two camps is not a notion that was imposed by literary historians but accurately reflects the self-perception of the Humanists, who began to consider themselves members of an intellectual community. Moreover, it was Johannes Reuchlin who became the acknowledged head of the republic of scholars. Young and old friends, close and remote acquaintances, identified with him, declaring their solidarity. For a while, the word *Reuchlinista* became a word of honor. Not all Humanists necessarily supported Reuchlin's Hebrew studies, but afraid that what happened to him might befall any of them, they rose up, willing and ready to defend the new learning against the hostility of the conservative theological establishment.

In 1518 a poem called *Triumphus Doctoris Reuchlini* was published in Tübingen. It was accompanied by a woodcut in which the victorious Humanist is shown entering his home town like an ancient *triumphator*. The weapons of the vanquished theologians are carried in front in a long line, headed by arguments of a thousand different kinds and as many sophistic conclusions. These are followed by the four main idols: Superstition, Barbarism, Ignorance, and Envy. Next, the enemies themselves appear, vanquished and chained: Hochstraten, Ortvin, Arnold von Tungern, and Pfefferkorn, followed by the victor himself, Reuchlin, preceded by sacrificial animals, music, and singers. Enthroned on a triumphal chariot, his head wreathed with laurel and ivy, he sits holding his *Augenspiegel* in his right hand. Bringing up the rear are all the jurists and poets who had been willing to fight and, if necessary, die at the stake for his cause.

Johannes Reuchlin was at the zenith of his fame. And so was German Humanism.

Chapter Five

The Flowering of Humanism: The Next Generation

Conradus Mutianus Rufus

His contemporaries mentioned Conradus Mutianus Rufus in the same breath with Reuchlin and Erasmus. Posterity, scarcely less enthusiastic, gave him fourth place after Luther, Reuchlin, and Erasmus—an impressive ranking considering the wealth of outstanding personalities living during this period. He corresponded with Reuchlin, Erasmus, and Pirckheimer, not to mention a host of lesser-known though by no means unimportant men, and was, without doubt, one of the greatest and most versatile scholars of the time. Just as three hundred years later visitors traveling through that part of Germany went to Weimar to pay their respects to Goethe, so did scholars at that era stop over at his house in Gotha to meet the famous Mutianus.

Mutianus's impact on other Humanists, which extended far beyond the circle of his Erfurt friends, can be compared to that of Rudolf Agricola. Yet Mutianus published even less than the Frisian Humanist: in fact, none of his works appeared in print. His refusal to publish is one of the peculiarities that has provoked much speculation among scholars. Was it his striving for unattainable stylistic perfection that prevented him from giving anything to the printer? Or was it an innate shyness, or a lack of conviction for his ideas, or even fear that his often unorthodox thoughts would offend people? He himself jokingly suggested that neither Christ nor Socrates ever published a word, and that he preferred to be entertained by the follies of others rather than by his own writings. But though he did not publish a single line, he composed numerous letters to his friends during the course of the years. And it is those letters, all written in Latin, that provide us with important insights into his life and thinking.[1]

Konrad Muth, or Conradus Mutianus Rufus, as he called himself in familiar Humanist fashion—he adopted the cognomen Rufus after the red color of his hair—was born in 1470 or 1471 in Homberg near Fritzlar in Hesse. His father was a popular city councillor; his mother came from a noble family. After attending the famous school of Deventer (Netherlands), which at that time was directed by Alexander Hegius, he enrolled at the University of Erfurt in 1486 and received his bachelor's and master's degrees in 1488 and 1492. With fondness he later remembered Conrad Celtis, who had taught there for some time. Erfurt was not only one of the oldest but also one of the most distinguished German universities, and it was an honor that Mutianus was invited to teach here after a while, apparently drawing large audiences. Soon after that, however, renouncing his academic career, he realized every Northern Humanist's dream: he crossed the Alps to go to Italy. Bologna, where he earned a doctor of law degree, Florence, Ferrara, and Rome were the main stages of his itinerary. For him, as for many others, this stay in Italy was of decisive importance, laying not only the foundation for his phenomenal knowledge of ancient literature, but also exposing him to a remarkable collection of men, among them Philipp Beroaldus and Baptista Mantuanus, the poet. What is more important, in Florence he came in contact with Marsilio Ficino and his neo-Platonic philosophy without which his theology is unthinkable.

When Mutianus returned to his native country after seven years in Italy, he served for a short time at the Hessian court, where his brother was chancellor. But having no taste for the courtly life he soon wrote the words "Valete sollicitudines" ("farewell, you cares")! on his office door and took leave (Gillert, xxiv). Through family connections he was able to secure a modest benefice in Gotha, a small town fourteen miles west of Erfurt. As canon of St. Mary's Church he was to spend the next quarter century there until his death in 1526.

Gotha was hardly a congenial place for a man who not only had been in contact with the newest ideas in Italy but also was deeply moved by his love for ancient literature and philosophy. His fellow canons, on the other hand, did not seem to be too responsive to the new learning. Outraged by the perfunctory performance of their religious duties as well as by their barbaric Latin, not to mention their immorality and corruption, Mutianus had only contempt for them, avoiding all opportunities for socializing. They in turn looked disapprovingly on his enthusiasm for pagan literature and noticed with some amazement that ten years had to pass before he celebrated mass for the first time.

Mutianus was nevertheless fortunate in finding a few friends with whom he could exchange ideas and pursue his classical studies. Soon his house became the center for this group of loyal companions. A sign reading *Beata Tranquillitas* ("Blessed Tranquillity") on the outside of that building suggested that here an island of quiet serenity and peace of mind had been created, while a similar sign inside saying *Bonis cuncta pateant* ("everything shall be open to the good") was an open invitation to all interested in convivial scholarship. One of Mutianus's most trusted friends was Heinrich Fastnacht from Orb (Latin: *Urba*) near Gelnhausen, who for that reason called himself Urbanus. Though not a writer himself, this monk from the nearby Cistercian monastery of Georgenthal must be credited with having preserved the letters his friend sent him daily, over the years, starting in 1505. Of the over six hundred letters written by Mutianus to different persons and preserved for us, more than half are addressed to Urbanus. Composed with wit, humor, and a wealth of classical allusions, these communications contain not only miniature lectures on fine points of scholarship but also commonplace discussions of down-to-earth matters, revealing the opposite temperaments of the two friends: Urbanus, who was overseer in that monastery, the pragmatic manager of large amounts of money, and Mutianus, who with his unstinting generosity, had a difficult time making ends meet. Frequently the latter had to make requests for cash advances, which his friend invariably granted. Knowing his friend's situation, Urbanus also occasionally volunteered to send large quantities of cheese and butter to the canon, who showed his gratitude by communicating all sorts of literary chitchat (Gillert, 1:70f.). For his friend, Mutianus was even willing to loosen his usually high moral standards a little. In 1508, for instance, Urbanus had a liaison with a young nun which resulted in the pregnant girl's flight from the convent. In a conversation with Urbanus's superior Mutianus tried to play down the entire affair, saying that his friend and the nun had just been chatting with each other. When the abbot pointed out the undeniable fact of the nun's pregnancy, Mutianus exclaimed, "Well, the old dilapidated wall around the convent should have been repaired!" (Gillert, 1:102f.).

Other members of the Humanist's inner circle were Georg Spalatin, a modest, almost timid young man, who later became a prominent Protestant reformer, the talented poet Eobanus Hessus, Peter Eberbach, Herbord von der Marthen, and Crotus Rubeanus, the author of the first part of the *Letters of Obscure Men*, who also introduced Ulrich von Hutten into the Gotha fraternity. Euricius Cordus and Joachim Camerarius were also later attracted to Gotha.

The dominant theme in all of Mutianus's letters is his love for the language and literature of ancient Greece and Rome. Far from being a remote field of study, antiquity was for him something very concrete and personal. Calling it "a marriageable and beautiful virgin," he found antiquity, as we recall, to be "ravishingly beautiful" and "without any blemishes." It was therefore painful for him to see that nobody wanted "to pull at her little ears and press lips to lips." To express it in less erotic terms, he deplored the fact that Humanist studies were neglected and that "Virgil, Cicero, and Livy were hungry, naked, and lacking food, dress, and shoes" (Gillert, 1:8). To provide food, clothing, and shelter for these ancient authors was the task of the *ordo latinus*, as he sometimes called the circle of his Humanist friends. In order to do that, a thorough familiarity with them was necessary, and Mutianus never tired of admonishing his students to study them carefully. Like a teacher, he gave his friends assignments which he then subjected to careful critiques.

The most important requirement for a study of the ancient authors, as for that of any authors, are books, and if the unassuming canon ever indulged in a passion, it was his love of books. His letters are filled with thoughts on how to obtain them, their quality, and, above all, their cost. In order to save the fee of the middleman, for instance, Mutianus and his close friends Urbanus and Spalatin, tried to order directly from Aldus Manutius in Venice. A good number of letters (Gillert, 1:18–22; 26; 29; 33–34; 34–37), all mutually criticized for style and accuracy, but full of ideas on this exciting business transaction were exchanged. When the order was finally placed, it turned out to be a fairly modest one. Aldus, however, was gracious enough to write to each of the three bibliophiles, encouraging them to continue with their studies. On another occasion Mutianus deplored the war in Italy for the sole reason that it interfered with the regular shipment of books from Venice.

If Mutianus and his friends were united in their love of classical antiquity, they were equally so in their fight against Scholasticism and orthodox theologians. Nowhere did this become clearer than in the Reuchlin affair. As early as 1503 Mutianus had written to Reuchlin, asking him for his friendship (Gillert, 1:2–3). When the question of the confiscation and possible destruction of the Jewish books arose, he promptly and unhesitatingly backed the scholar from Pforzheim without even having seen the latter's famous legal brief. He maintained this position of unreserved support throughout the controversy, writing in 1512:

A grasshopper will rather give birth to a Lucanian [i.e., an elephant] than I will change my mind about Reuchlin. Never have I attempted to investigate the evil deeds of other people, but now time admonishes me to pick out the eyes of the crows. Pythagoras taught his students to be silent. Therefore, like a Pythagorean, I held my tongue thus far. But when a most learned man is attacked and a base renegade [Pfefferkorn] is defended, I will do everything in my power to help him—not as an advocate for the Jews—I don't presume to be that—but as a defender of Johannes Reuchlin, who out of love for the truth, has written a just legal brief about the Talmudic books . . . (Gillert, 1:303f.)

There is no point in detailing here, year by year, his stance in this drawn-out controversy. But his keen interest in and concern for Reuchlin's cause is reflected in his correspondence during these years, and it is well to remember that both the *Triumphus Capnionis* [The triumph of Reuchlin] and the *Letters of Obscure Men* originated in Mutianus's circle, although he himself, given his aversion to public literary activity, probably had no direct part in the writing of the satire.

As the undisputed head of the Erfurt Humanists (though he was not officially a member of the University of Erfurt, it claimed him as one of theirs) Mutianus's reputation rested mainly on his vast knowledge of classical antiquity. It would be wrong, however, to regard him primarily as a classical philologist. As a matter of fact, he resented being compared to Cicero—a comparison many of his peers would not have minded—but wished to be considered a *philosophus sanctus*, or, to use a more modern term, a theological philosopher or philosophical theologian. On the surface, this looks like

a singularly inappropriate name for a man whose letters reveal not
only a persistent distaste for the outward manifestations of the Church
but also a deep skepticism about the essence of Christianity. His
attacks on priests, for instance, are frequent and sharp:

The illiterate priests, who have hardly tasted the rudiments of learning
with the tips of their tongues, pronounce words so barbarously, so cor-
ruptedly that they defile Christian ceremonies with indelible stains. But
that would be tolerable if they only sinned with their language and were
not contaminated by all sorts of disgraceful behavior and depraved in their
mouths as well as in their minds. They have no fear of God; there is
nothing deeply religious about them except their priestly garb. They are
not interested in the Savior, nor in virtue nor in an orderly, chaste, and
quiet life, but they indulge in sex and worship the stomach, and what is
below it. They are always quarrelsome, always drunk. (Gillert, 1:213).

In addition to attacking the corrupted clergy, he constantly as-
saulted religious customs like fasting, confession, and mandatory
attendance of religious services. Himself of frail health, he remarked
on fasting: "The powers of body and soul have to be strengthened
through food and drink. Fasting produces emaciation, dulling the
mind rather than sharpening it" (Krause, xxv). The real motive for
the obligation to fast, Mutianus further suggested, is the greed of
the clergy. If they had not invented fasting, the farmers would keep
their chicken and eggs for themselves and not donate them to the
Church. Fasting and religious penance laws, especially auricular
confession, are powerful weapons in the hands of the priests who
want to frighten the souls and bring them under their power, he
maintained. "The priests are not content with plaguing the body
with fasting. They also castigate the souls by rebuking the people
for their sins. While the Homeric donkey grazes quietly on the
meadow without letting himself be chased away by the shepherd's
stick, people let themselves be frightened by terrible-sounding words"
(Gillert, 2:8). These remarks cannot be dismissed as a piece of
whimsical humor. They are in fact a perceptive analysis of the social
situation of the time, undertaken by a man who was himself a priest.

Mutianus expressed himself equally scornfully about other forms
of ecclesiastical piety. The murmuring of prayers and the habits of
monks and nuns as well as the worship of relics are all calculated,
according to him, to take advantage of the primitive superstition
of the common people and to satisfy the priestly greed. In another

letter he commented on two wealthy canons who turned to their "gods" during an attack on Erfurt. "The fools believe that statues and pictures can protect them and others" (Krause, 205). Nor did he spare the worship of "golden relics," as he called them, especially the Holy Coat of Trier which had been newly exhibited in 1512. For him that was not only a superstition, but a profitable one for the priests (Krause, 438). "What I think of bones you know," he wrote to Urbanus. "Christ detests lies, but nobody lies more blatantly than Christ's priests" (Krause, 427).

There was of course nothing unusual about these attacks on the Church and her representatives; they were quite common during the pre-Reformation era. What was remarkable, however, was the sharpness and clarity of Mutianus's analysis, which uncovered a system of deliberate exploitation practiced by the Church. The fact that he expressed these politically and socially explosive ideas in private letters to friends with the frequently expressed injunction "*Concerpe!*" ("Tear it up!") does not detract from their revolutionary character.

Yet though his ideas might seem extremely modern, Mutianus was neither an eighteenth-century rationalist nor a twentieth-century Marxist, but a deeply religious man. But his religiosity was of a very unorthodox kind. Drawing liberally on the neo-Platonic philosophy he had studied during his stay in Florence, he believed that the essence of things was the spirit. As the body is only the slave of the spirit, everything physical is only the insignificant dress of the eternal spirit which manifests itself in the different religions. The various aspects of this manifestation of the divine could be seen from the different names given to it. In a letter to Urbanus Mutianus wrote:

There is one god and one goddess, but there are as many deities as there are names [*sed sunt multa ut numina ita et nomina*], for instance, Jupiter, the Sun, Apollo, Moses, Christ, the Moon, Ceres, Proserpina, the Earth, and Mary. But be careful not to say this aloud for it must be concealed, hidden in silence like the mysteries of the Eleusinian goddesses. In religion everything is couched in the form of fables and riddles. You despise with the help of Jupiter, that is the highest God, the smaller gods. When I say Jupiter, I mean Christ and the true God. (Gillert, 1:23)

By identifying the ancient gods with the Christian God, Mutianus established a bridge between classical antiquity and Christianity.

In one breath he prayed to Luna Lucina and Saint Lucia. Saint Benedict was called Pythagoras, and the sun, Sol, was termed the father of all men and gods. Mutianus therefore found traces of Christianity in the oldest times. To him God's wisdom revealed itself not only with the Jews but also with the ancient Greeks, Romans, and Germans (Gillert, 1:137). In view of this spiritualization of his religion, it was only logical that for him Christ's human nature was of secondary significance since the true man was not he who was physically visible, but his spirit. In all seriousness he once maintained that he was present at a mass celebrated by Spalatin, present not in body, to be sure, but in mind (Gillert, 1:149).

Mutianus's views of the spiritual nature of Christianity also determined his ethics. Not the strict observance of man-made rules was important for him but good and just conduct:

The usual donations of external sacrifices to the Church are not pleasing to God. The real offerings, however, are blessed tranquillity, a mild heart, an innocent life, and good actions. God does not want wheat bread, sacrificial cake or animals, candles, cheese, eggs, money, or empty prayers. On the altar should be placed what is in the heart of man: justice, faith, innocence, chastity, abstinence, and the rest of the virtues. No religion is truer, no law holier than that which teaches us to live justly and properly. This is true religious worship. This is Christ's magnificent, divine, and eternal dogma. These teachings are contained in the Gospel which came from the schools of the Hebrews, Epicureans, and Stoics. (Krause, 460)

At the same time Mutianus's letters reveal a deplorable double standard and a sense of elitism. For him only the philosopher was allowed to indulge in such ideas, as long as he kept them to himself. The majority of the people, on the other hand, had to be deceived through religion and laws. The authority of the Church, in spite of its imperfections, has to be preserved, since without it everything would result in chaos and brute force (Krause, 353). In light of this inconsistency it is not surprising to learn that Mutianus accommodated himself rather well to the external forms of the Church: "I am murmuring with those who murmur lest I be accused of impiety." Or: "I live holy with the holy men, read the Hebrew commentaries, and give the gods their due" (Krause, 150). In the controversy of Locher against Zingel and Wimpfeling (cf. chap. 3) he therefore sided publicly with the theologians, saying that the secrets of theologians should not be profaned. Priests, he further maintained, should not read any poems except those of the pious Baptista Mantuanus.

The same unresolved dualism can be found in Mutianus's attitude toward the Reformation. There were obviously many views he shared with Luther, such as his impatience with ecclesiastical abuses and his aversion to the clergy as mediators between the individual and God. For this reason, he was, at least initially, a supporter of Luther. But when he became aware of the wider ramifications of the reform movement and the subsequent social and political unrest, he turned into an opponent of the Reformer and his cause.

Mutianus's last years were spent in loneliness and misery. His *Beata Tranquillitas* was no longer the center for social gatherings of Humanists and poets. A touching appeal for help to his benefactor, the Protestant Elector Frederick the Wise, reveals more than any other document the personal tragedy into which the social, religious, and political upheavals had drawn him and many other Humanists: "My prince and unvanquished king! Saddened to death is my soul . . . I, wretched, aging and graying, am forced to go begging . . . In your Gotha, benign father, where I lived an innocent life for twenty-three years, where I did not offend anybody and helped those I could, here I would like to grow old. But I will be without the necessities of life. The income of the benefices is abolished. What should I, poor man, live on? . . . Let me have bread and some money for victuals" (Gillert, 2:306ff.).

Since the Elector died a few weeks later, it is doubtful that he ever read this letter. Mutianus himself passed away a year later, on Good Friday, 1526. Nobody mourned his death more deeply than his most gifted student, Crotus Rubeanus. He wrote, "Mutianus's death has been the most bitter to me, next to that of my parents. Nobody's friendship was ever dearer to me, nobody's soul was ever closer to me than his" (Krause, lxv).

Willibald Pirckheimer

Thanks to the artistic skill of Albrecht Dürer, posterity has a very good idea of what Willibald Pirckheimer looked like.[2] We see a mighty head framed by fairly long, shaggy but well-ordered hair. The face is dominated by big, intelligent eyes. The mighty broken nose and sensually thick lips suggest a certain roguishness, while the chin, jutting out a little but not unpleasantly, gives him an air of determination. The fleshy neck is partly covered by an expensive fur. It is the head of a self-confident man who knows who he is and how to enjoy life.

Pirckheimer was the scion of a well-to-do patrician Nuremberg family, which had combined their commercial activities with intellectual pursuits.[3] Both Willibald's grandfather and father had studied in Italy; indeed, his father had even earned a doctor of law degree in the South. It was this promotion, however, which prohibited him from serving on the city council of Nuremberg according to a statute in the constitution of that community. It may have been this exclusion from active participation in town government that prompted the older Pirckheimer to leave the city and try to make his fortune elsewhere. With his family he moved to Eichstätt, a small but at that time important city about thirty-eight miles south of Nuremberg. Here Willibald was born in 1470 and spent the first five years of his life. In 1488 his father, in the meantime counselor to the Bishop of Eichstätt and later to Albrecht IV of Bavaria and the Archduke Sigmund of Tyrolia, sent him to Padua for the purpose of studying law. Like many of his fellow students, he was more attracted to the *studia humanitatis* than to dry legal studies. Greek especially interested him, and in Padua his impressive knowledge of that language was established. But he also became intrigued by Aristotelian and Platonic philosophy, as well as by the natural sciences, mathematics, geography, and medicine.

When his father learned about the scope of his interests, he asked Willibald to transfer to Pavia in order to concentrate on legal studies, a request with which young Pirckheimer dutifully complied. Although Willibald's intention was to earn the doctor of law degree and then enter the service of the emperor, his father, having himself experienced the dangers of court life, dissuaded him from this plan, recommending instead that he return to Nuremberg and devote himself to the service of that city. He was even thoughtful enough to choose a wife for his son from an impeccably patrician family. Thus, after seven years in Italy, young Willibald returned to Germany in 1495 without an academic degree and was soon afterwards elected to the city council, on which he served, with an interruption between 1502 and 1505, until 1523.

At that time Nuremberg was a thriving city, the second largest in the empire, whose praises Eyb and Celtis had sung. The wealth of its citizens had also brought on an impressive cultural flowering.

In addition to Albrecht Dürer, the city could boast of such prominent artists as Adam Krafft, Veit Stoss, and Peter Fischer. Hans Sachs was fixing shoes and writing poems in the "jewel of the empire," as the city was often called, and Christoph Scheuerl, a well-known Nuremberg citizen, could exclaim, "God be thanked that I was born as a man, not as a woman, as a citizen of Nuremberg and not as an Italian." That he expressed these proud sentiments in a speech at the University of Bologna is all the more remarkable. Relations between these self-confident Nurembergers and Pirckheimer were somewhat strained. There were too many features in his character that made it difficult to work smoothly with him. He could be stubborn, dogmatic, opinionated, and hot-tempered. In 1507, for instance, he was fined and sent to prison for two days for slapping two citizens from Donauwörth in the face. Occasionally he was reprimanded for irregular attendance at the city council meetings or for interrupting the speakers. His absence in 1502 for three years was due to a bitter dispute with certain of his fellow councillors. Furthermore, in 1514 Hans Schütz, who had been exiled from Nuremberg because of his debts, published a libellous work blaming Pirckheimer for his misfortunes and accusing him of a variety of offenses, including the charge that the Humanist was "chasing women and virgins." Though the latter eloquently refuted most of these accusations, he passed over the allegations concerning his amatory life in curious silence. That was probably the wisest thing to do. For after the death of his wife, who had given birth to six children within seven years of marriage, Pirckheimer chose not to remarry, preferring instead a merry widowerhood. That he did not scorn the pleasures of the flesh emerges with great clarity from his correspondence with his close friends Dürer and Lorenz Behaim.

Interminably long council meetings, unpleasant frictions with fellow citizens, participation in military campaigns, and stormy love affairs (which at least in one case resulted in the birth of an illegitimate son) made up one side of Pirckheimer's life. But in addition and parallel to it, he created for himself a quieter existence, the world of his Humanist studies. Expanding the sizable collection of books he had inherited from his family, he built up one of the largest private libraries in Germany. Although Mutianus fussed over a book order to Aldus Manutius for weeks, the Nuremberg Humanist treated such a purchase from the Venetian printer as a routine

matter. Like Mutianus, he generously extended his hospitality to
scholars, but unlike the canon of Gotha, he could afford it. His
house thus became the meeting place, or, as Celtis put it, the
"hospice" for Humanists. He was admired, his company was sought
after, and offers for exchange of letters were made. Celtis, Reuchlin,
Hutten, Melanchthon, and Erasmus, as well as a host of minor
personalities, were his correspondents. A number of younger Humanists, like Johann Cochlaeus, Eobanus Hessus, and Joachim Camerarius, were decisively influenced by him.

Pirckheimer's interests were far-ranging and by no means confined
to literature. Fascinated by physics, alchemy, medicine, geography,
and theology, he also collected ancient coins and inscriptions. The
breadth of his interests is indicated by his many translations from
Greek into Latin or from both ancient languages into German, as
well as editions of Greek and Latin works. Among those Greek
authors whose works he rendered into Latin, Lucian was Pirckheimer's favorite. What appealed to him in the works of this Greek
rhetorician and satirist was the latter's fight against superstition,
fraud, and arrogance as well as his skeptical and Epicurean tendencies. Another Greek author to whom Pirckheimer was particularly attracted was Plutarch, whose treatises on ethical and moral
questions he translated. A considerable part of his activity as translator was also devoted to the rendering of early Greek Church fathers,
patristic authors, like Nilus, Fulgentius, and Gregory of Nazians.
At the request of Emperor Maximilan, the Nuremberg Humanist
further translated the *Hieroglyphica* [Hieroglyphics] of the Egyptian
Horapollon, a task that was considered especially difficult and for
which he engaged Dürer as an illustrator. Just as Reuchlin had
opened up the world of Jewish thought, Pirckheimer brought the
Orient and Egypt into the field of vision of the German Renaissance
with this translation.[4]

Though his well-known liaisons might have contributed to Pirckheimer's failure to attain the highest offices in the Nuremberg city
administration, his fellow councillors were judicious enough to draw
on his extraordinary talents and employed him on various diplomatic
and military missions. The most famous of these was his participation as field captain in the Swiss War of 1499. Basically a clash
between the Hapsburg dynasty and the Swiss Confederates, this
particular conflict was caused by a number of factors, including the
refusal of the Swiss to pay the newly instituted imperial tax, the

so-called "common penny," and to recognize the new Imperial Court (*Reichskammergericht*). Nuremberg was called upon to join the imperial forces in this campaign, which the peaceful Swiss themselves prefer to call the "Swabian war," because it was initially fought between them and the Swabian League. Without much enthusiasm, for fear of jeopardizing their excellent trade relations, the Nurembergers raised a troop of four hundred foot-soldiers and sixty horsemen, and put Pirckheimer in charge of this contingent. Lasting from February to August of 1499, the hostilities ended with the Peace of Basel, in which the Swiss were virtually granted independence, although *de iure* they belonged to the German Empire until 1648, when the Treaty of Westphalia was concluded.

Important as this war was politically both for the Swiss and the empire, it was also significant for literary history because it inspired Pirckheimer's intelligent and sensitive account, his *Bellum Helveticum* [Swiss war].[5] In the first of the two books he sketches the background of Swiss history prior to the outbreak of the war in order to explain the mentality of the rebels. In this part, the Nuremberg Humanist relied mainly on a Swiss chronicle written in German by Petermann Etterlin entitled *Kronika von der löblichen Eidgenossenschaft* [Chronicle of the praiseworthy Swiss confederacy], which he, of course, translated into Latin. The second book deals with the immediate causes of the war and its actual course. Since Pirckheimer entered the theater of war in the middle of the conflict and then only in a somewhat subordinate function, he had to rely heavily on hearsay reports in addition to Etterlin's chronicle.

Coming from Pirckheimer, the *Bellum Helveticum* has naturally all the trappings of a Humanist work. Written in Latin, it is not only filled with appropriate quotes from Cicero and Sallust on the value of historiography but is also imbued with that patriotic spirit that is so characteristic of the historical writing of German Humanists. But what makes it worthwhile reading even today, in addition to its being a valuable historical source, are the vivid eyewitness accounts, which clearly reveal Pirckheimer's sensitivity and personal involvement. Moreover, although not blind to the bravery of the soldiers, he also describes the suffering of the civilian population with sympathy. For a twentieth-century reader familiar with the cruelties of war these episodes might well be the most touching ones. In the following passage he describes the pain of innocent children:

During my march I happened to come through a large but burnt-down village. At the end of it I discovered two old women driving before them a crowd of about forty boys and girls like a herd of cattle. Totally emaciated from starvation, they frightened any passerby by their very appearance. I asked the old women where they were taking this pitiful group. And although they were bewildered and hardly able to open their mouths from pain and hunger, they answered that I would soon see myself where they were leading these unhappy children. Hardly had they said this, when the boys and girls came to a meadow, where they fell down on their knees and started to eat up the herbs like animals, differing from those only by picking the food with their hands while animals bite it off. Through experience they had already learned to distinguish the herbs, knowing which ones were bitter and inedible and which sweet and tasty. They especially picked out sorrel preferring it to all other herbs. I was as if turned to stone at such a sorry sight and remained there, bereft of reason, for a long time. Again one of those old women said, "Don't you see why these unhappy children were taken here. It would have been better for them if they had never been born than to be exposed to these sufferings and to lead such a wretched life. Swords killed their fathers, hunger their mothers, their possessions were looted, their houses burnt. We miserable women were spared because of our extreme old age" . . . When I had seen and heard this, I could not hold back my tears. I felt pity with the sad fate of these people and cursed the madness of war.[6]

The final draft of the *Bellum Helveticum* was not finished until thirty years after Pirckheimer's participation in it, showing clearly that it took him that long to cope with the deep emotional experience of that conflict. The same reason might have made him hesitate to publish it during his life. It was not printed until 1610, eighty years after his death.

Pirckheimer's only major literary work that appeared during his life was the *Apologia seu Laus Podagrae* [The defense or praise of the gout]. As with the *Swiss War*, personal interest and involvement were the decisive factors inspiring the composition of this work. In this case the involvement was a rather painful one for he had suffered from attacks of this disease since 1512. In the absence of effective medication, it became more severe as he grew older, forcing him, for instance, to cover the very short distance between his house and the city council chambers in Nuremberg on horseback. According to medical opinion prevalent at that time, gout was blamed on overeating, drinking, and sex, or, as the age, given more to allegories, put it, "Bacchus is the father, Venus the mother, and Luxuria the midwife. The child is called Podagra, or Gout." And in fact Pirckheimer was not known to be an ascetic in any of these categories.[7] He himself laid the blame for his affliction on less hedonistic occupations, ascribing it instead to emotional stress and assiduous studying.

This charming little work, repeatedly reprinted and translated into German and English, was inspired by Lucian's dramatic joke *Tragipodagra*, in which an entire chorus of podagrists, or goutsufferers, sings the praises of their mighty mistress, as well as by Erasmus's *Praise of Folly* (cf. 112). The idea is the following: a female figure, Podagra, or Gout, is summoned to an imaginary court by the many persons who are subjected to her cruel domination. Brilliantly defending herself, she says: "Those who accuse me of wrongdoing are themselves to blame. Rarely do I come on my own accord but always forced. I don't enjoy tough and hardened people who never take a rest, who constantly exercise their bodies through work and activity, who never or rarely indulge, suffer hunger, eat simple food, quench their thirst with water, wear simple dresses, sleep in even simpler beds, and renounce all pleasures."[8] Having conveniently shifted the blame on to her victims, Podagra proceeds to point out that the evils she is accused of are not as bad as they are made out to be, and that she in fact brings a number of obvious benefits and advantages to her victims. For instance, if you are stricken with gout, you cannot go to sea, but when you cannot go to sea, the Gout argues with impeccable logic, you cannot expose yourself to the dangers of drowning. Nor does one have to be afraid of the dangers of hunting, or walking, or falling roof tiles—apparently not an infrequent occurrence in old Nuremberg—if one is bedridden.

If you cannot exercise your body, Podagra continues, you exercise your mind. She therefore also takes credit for the study of languages, music, rhetoric, astronomy, etc., as well as that of medical books. All of this shows, according to her, how unselfish she really is; for medical research, based on books of course, might reveal how to get rid of her. Her speech culminates in the praise of gout because it directs the attention away from the physical toward the spiritual and eternal: "These silly people don't know that through their accusations they praise rather than insult me, for while I weaken the body, I heal the mind; while I debilitate the flesh, I strengthen the soul; while I dispel the earthly, I introduce divine things; while I take away all things transient, I bring the eternal."[9]

Although the varied relationships between German Humanists and artists are outside the scope of this book, brief mention must be made of the lifelong and fruitful friendship between one of Germany's outstanding representatives of the new learning, Pirckheimer, and its greatest artist of that time, Albrecht Dürer. Like any genuine friendship, theirs was one of a generous give and take. Each was able to offer something the other did not possess. Apart from being helped financially in his difficult years by Pirckheimer, Dürer became acquainted with numerous descriptions of ancient works of art and could draw on his friend's vast knowledge of Greek and Roman literature, philosophy, and mythology. Pirckheimer, in turn, received book illustrations, ex libris, and portraits of himself, including the famous copper engraving mentioned at the beginning of this section.

Their cooperation resulted in three works, all sponsored by Emperor Maximilian. The first of these joint labors was the already mentioned *Hieroglyphics* of Horapollon, a work to which the emperor had been drawn because of his interest in emblems. Pirckheimer translated the work from Greek into Latin, while his artist friend provided the illustrations. Though without much value to the modern Egyptologist because of its numerous misconceptions and fanciful explanations, the work is interesting to the student of Humanism and the Baroque because of the many inspirations it provided for the emblem literature of the sixteenth and seventeenth centuries.[10]

Allegories and emblematics were also dominant concepts in the next work of the two friends, the *Ehrenpforte* [Triumphal arch], a mammoth verbo-visual glorification of the Hapsburg dynasty and Maximilian, who had commissioned a number of artists and authors with the execution of that project, among them Pirckheimer and Dürer. Both men were also won by the emperor for his *Triumphzug* [Triumphal procession], again a self-glorification of the Hapsburgs. This time, however, their involvement was confined to one part of the total work, the so-called *Der Grosse Triumphwagen* [Great triumphal chariot], representing probably the most significant example of their collaboration. The emperor honored both men in his own way for their work. Pirckheimer was appointed imperial councillor, while Dürer received an annuity of one hundred guilders. The funds for this stipend, however, were to be taken out of the taxes paid by the city of Nuremberg. Maximilian's generosity had definite limits.

In light of their almost daily association, Dürer's death in 1528 was probably the most painful loss in Pirckheimer's life, prompting him to write his "Elegia Bilibaldi Pirckheymeri in obitum Alberti Düreri" [Willibald Pirckheimer's èlegy on the death of Albrecht Dürer]. It is not only one of the most touching but also one of the best poems of German Humanism—a somewhat surprising assessment since we usually do not associate poetry with Pirckheimer's name. Although he had written some poems of undistinguished quality in his youth, he later gratified his lyrical muse only rarely. Yet on this one occasion, toward the end of his life, driven by the intensity of his pain, he succeeded in crafting a work that stood head and shoulders above many a poem written by his professional colleagues. The basic mood is one of intense anguish over the loss of a close friend and outstanding artist, coupled with the conviction that death is only a temporary matter:

You who, for so many years, of my friends were the most intimate one,
    Albrecht, and of my soul the better, more valuable part,
with whom I could hold delightful conversations,
    certain that I would sow my words in a trustworthy heart.
Why, of a sudden, do you leave your mourning friend,
    hastening away, unfortunate man, with quick steps, never to return?
It was not granted to me to touch your dear head, to take your right hand,
    bidding a grievous farewell, dear friend, in mourning to you.
Hardly had you laid down your weary limbs on a camp bed
    when in a haste savage Death suddenly snatched you away.
Oh, false hopes of men, and hearts unaware of the evils,
    how in the wink of a moment everything suddenly falls!
All he wanted to have kind fortune had given to Dürer:
    power and genius to paint, honesty, unswerving faith.
But with a quick snatch Death tore away everything;
    only fame and renown cannot be wiped out by him.
Dürer's art will remain and so will his time-honored glory,
    as long as the bright stars will wander the skies . . . [11]

Although Pirckheimer remained aloof from the Reuchlin affair at first, he later clearly supported the Humanist from Pforzheim. Possibly stung by the unflattering reference to him as "a certain unknown Willibald" emanating from the Cologne theologians and convinced that their narrow-minded attack on Hebrew books was a threat to all Humanists, he published in 1517 his *Defensio Reuchlini* as a preface to his Latin translation of Lucian's *Piscator seu Reviviscentes* [The fisherman or the resurrected philosophers], a defense that was well received by the other Humanists.

Far less unequivocal was his attitude toward Luther and the Reformation. Like many other Humanists, he initially welcomed the new forces of religious dissent but had reservations and even misgivings when he saw the cultural and social consequences of the movement. Against his will he became involved in a bitter controversy almost at the very beginning of the Reformation. In July, 1519, Luther and Dr. Johann Eck, a theology professor from Ingolstadt and a staunch defender of the old faith and the papacy, engaged in a heated theological disputation at the University of Leipzig. As happens so often on these occasions, each claimed victory. In the eyes of Eck and his followers Luther had been unmasked as a religious radical, who claimed that in matters of faith the only authority he recognized was the Bible. Luther's supporters, on the other hand, saw in Eck the representative of the old Scholastic theology who had to be opposed with all means. In the aftermath of this debate there appeared a satire on Eck entitled *Eccius Dedolatus* [Eck planed down]. Brilliantly written and full of witty allusions to classical authors, it is probably the best Reformation satire and one of the gems of that genre in German literature. [12]

Though the satire appeared under the pseudonym "Joannefranciscus Cotta Lembergius," most contemporaries, including Eck, considered Pirckheimer its author. A month after the appearance of *Eccius Dedolatus* the Ingolstadt theologian (Eck) went to Rome to press his case against Luther and his followers, drafting the papal bull "Exsurge Domine" in which the German reformer (Luther) was threatened with excommunication unless he retracted the forty-one articles listed in it. Furthermore, Eck was given the right to include in this bull other names he considered favorable to the Lutheran cause. Seizing this opportunity to revenge himself against his hated opponent, Eck also cited Pirckheimer in addition to six other Protestants for "praising and exaggerating Luther's erroneous and misleading doctrines." [13] Though Pirckheimer recanted within the grace period, Eck intentionally or inadvertently failed to forward this information to Rome so that Pirckheimer was excommunicated. And although he was eventually absolved in the spring of 1524,

Eck had achieved what he wanted: he had thoroughly humiliated his opponent.

There is, however, clear evidence, too complicated to be detailed here, suggesting that, as Pirckheimer grew older, and as he saw the fruits of the Reformation movement, he regarded it with more and more misgivings.[14] Neither a good Protestant nor a good Catholic, he was too much his own man, too complicated, too scholarly, and too skeptical to accept blindly either the old faith or the new Protestant creed. Furthermore, he was not a theologian but a Christian layman who wanted to employ the wisdom of the ancient authors for reform and moral rejuvenation.

Not through the polemical works written during the Reformation but through his solid editions of ancient works, through his numerous translations, and through his original works, both in prose and verse, Pirckheimer will be remembered as one of Germany's outstanding Humanists. Under the famous copper engraving of his friend, Dürer wrote in Latin: "Vivitur ingenio—caetera mortis erunt" ("Man lives through his creative spirit—the rest will be gone with death"). The great Renaissance artist could not have chosen a more fitting motto.

Erasmus of Rotterdam

When, in the spring of 1484, Rudolf Agricola visited his friend Alexander Hegius, who had been appointed principal of the school in Deventer in the previous year, the latter proudly showed him some of the works of his pupils. There was Konrad Muth from Hesse (Mutianus), Hermann von dem Busche from Westphalia, and Geert Geertsz from Rotterdam, whose work Agricola liked best. He asked to see the boy. Quickly the fifteen-year-old lad recited a Latin poem he had written. After a long conversation following this recitation, the older Humanist dismissed the boy with the words, "You will become a great man."[15]

Agricola's prediction proved right. Of all the Northern Humanists Geert Geertsz, who in the manner of his learned contemporaries later latinized his name into Erasmus Desiderius Roterodamus, became undoubtedly the greatest. Through his *Adages, Colloquies*, and *The Praise of Folly*, his name became a household word all over Europe. When today someone speaks of Northern Humanism, his name is the first and, in many instances, the only one that comes to mind.

In his own day Erasmus enjoyed unrivaled popularity. Invitations came to him from all sides. Henry VII invited him to England, Francis I sent him a personal note requesting his company in Paris, Cardinal Ximenes offered him a position at the University of Alcala in Spain, the Duke of Saxony tried to lure him to Leipzig, and the universities of Cambridge, Oxford, Louvain, Basel, and Vienna vied for his presence. Especially the Germans, calling him Germany's ornament, showered him with honors. His trip up the Rhine in 1514 resembled a triumphal tour. Honored at banquets in Strasbourg and Basel, he was presented in Schlettstadt with three casks of the very finest wine—and the Alsatian wines were, and still are, known for their superb taste. His letters, of which three thousand are still extant, became collector's items in his own time. The Swiss theologian Oecolampadius, for instance, framed one and hung it over his desk—only to have it stolen by another Erasmus fan.[16]

Since there is no dearth of biographies in English, we can confine ourselves to a brief sketch of Erasmus's life. The Dutch Humanist was born in Rotterdam in 1466 or 1469 as the illegitimate son of a priest. In light of the generally solid documentation of his life, the uncertainty of his birthdate is somewhat surprising, giving headaches to Erasmus specialists as well as to those cultural functionaries responsible for organizing commemorative celebrations for the great man. Because the country of Holland in which Rotterdam was situated had retained its linguistic and cultural ties to the German Empire, although politically it belonged to Burgundy since the middle of the fifteenth century, the Germans have always claimed him as one of theirs. The Dutch, of course, whose country became a sovereign state only much later, can with equal right lay claim to him. Erasmus himself would have been puzzled and angered by this debate over his nationality. He had declared, after all, that the whole universe was his fatherland.

There is no doubt, however, that his prestige among the Germans was the greatest and that, at least after 1514, he frequently talked about *Germania nostra* ("our Germany"). It is with both his stature among the German Humanists and his identification with their cause in mind, that I include him somewhat hesitatingly in this survey of German Humanism.

After attending the school in Deventer, Erasmus entered the monastery of the Augustinian canon regulars in Steyn near Gouda in 1487. He took the vows one year later and was ordained in 1492.

A position as secretary to the Bishop of Cambrai gave him an opportunity to leave the monastery. His hope, however, of traveling to Rome with his new employer was shattered. Instead he went to the University of Paris to study theology (1495–1499). At the invitation of one of the wealthy British students he had tutored in Paris, he went to England (in 1499) where he met Thomas More and John Colet, beginning a lifelong friendship with these two eminent scholars. The years after his return from the British Isles were mostly spent in the Low Countries. After his second stay in England (1505–1506) he journeyed to Italy, where he was not only promoted to Doctor of Theology in Turin but also made the acquaintance of Aldus Manutius, the famous printer in Venice. After yet another sojourn in England, he returned once again to the Continent, establishing close relations with the southwest German Humanists and the Basel printer Johann Froben. The years 1517–1521 were passed mainly in Louvain, which he had to leave, however, in 1521 because of his refusal to take an unequivocal stand against Luther and his followers. A similar fate befell him eight years later in Basel. Because of the religious intolerance of the Protestants, he left this city and settled in nearby Freiburg, which had remained Catholic. After six years he returned once again to Basel where the religious fervor had somewhat subsided. Here he died in 1536.

This is obviously a mere sketch of Erasmus's life and it ignores not only the frequent travels he undertook—so frequent that he once joked that his horse must be the wisest in Europe because it had attended so many universities—but also the development of his mind, his stupendous erudition, and his attitude toward that epoch-making event, the Reformation. I will try to deal briefly with these aspects in the following pages.

Though today Erasmus's fame rests chiefly on *The Praise of Folly*—a work he later regretted having published—it was as a scholar that he was most admired during his own lifetime. Almost all his scholarly works reflect his attempt to synthesize the two cultural forces with which he was preoccupied throughout his life: the pagan antiquity of the Greeks and Romans and the culture of the Christian church fathers. Unlike many of his colleagues in theology and also unlike some of the more conservative Humanists such as Wimpfeling and Brant, he strongly advocated the study of the pagan authors. As a matter of fact, in one of his first works, the *Anti-barbari* [Anti-barbarians, 1493, published, 1520] he openly declared war on the enemies of classical learning. According to Erasmus the "anti-barbarians," united in their love for the *bonae literae*—a term he consistently used in lieu of *studia humanitatis*—wonder whether it is not possible to take Cicero and Horace as models and still be good Christians. It is significant that Erasmus thought of these authors not only as stylistic models but also as moral exemplars. He therefore considered it his duty as a Humanist and reformer to familiarize the reading public with the wisdom of the ancients. Certainly the best-known efforts in this direction are his *Adagia* [Adages], a collection of Latin, and later, in expanded editions, Greek sayings and proverbs, mostly drawn from ancient literature.[17]

The initial impulse for compiling the *Adagia* was a minor mishap Erasmus suffered on his return from his first stay in England in 1500. A law at that time forbade the export of money from Britain. Following the advice of his English friends, who assured him that in his case an exception would be made, the Dutch Humanist tried to take a considerable amount of cash out of the country. The exception was not made, however, and all of his funds were confiscated by the unimpressed British customs officials. Having vented his wrath about such unworthy treatment in numerous letters, the now-penniless scholar set out to earn some money quickly. It was under these circumstances that he conceived the idea of putting together a collection of Latin sayings. Though compared with later editions, the initial printing of 1500, with its approximately eight hundred sayings, was fairly modest; it nevertheless brought its author considerable fame and, more important, the desired monetary return.

The circumstances of the genesis of the second edition are equally interesting. In 1507 Erasmus stayed in the house of Aldus Manutius, which had become a center for the printing of Greek books and where the enthusiasm for Greek culture was so pronounced that everyone had to speak that language on pain of a fine. Generously supplied with Greek sayings and proverbs by the many native scholars who had gathered here, Erasmus, amidst the din of the printing presses, worked so feverishly on this new edition that he had hardly time "to scratch his ears," as he jokingly said. The result, published in 1508, was a vastly expanded edition which had grown to over three thousand sayings. What was remarkable about it was not only that it had quadrupled in size but also that now the Hellenic world was included, providing us with an index of Erasmus's widened intellectual horizon. With its greater scope, the object of the compilation had also changed. Not satisfied with merely listing and defining the proverbs, the Dutch Humanist also discussed their development, changes in meaning, and applicability to the present, using them often as pegs for longer essays on certain aspects of the ancient world or for commentaries on moral problems.

Up to his death Erasmus repeatedly revised and expanded the *Adagia*. Because of their wide distribution, they had an incalculable impact on the intellectual climate of the sixteenth century. By disseminating Humanist learning to a large and educated public all over Europe and familiarizing it with the world of ancient culture, Erasmus contributed to making Humanism less an affair of an exclusive circle of scholars than one of wider social groups. Through subsequent translations many of these sayings also entered various languages, including English. Here are a few examples: "stirring up a hornet's nest"—"to leave no stone unturned"—"to mix fire with water"—"with one foot in the grave"—"a rare bird"—"birds of a feather flock together"—"where there is smoke there is fire."

While the *Adagia* offered a great panorama of Greek and Roman antiquity, they also introduced many people to the world of the Latin and Greek Church fathers, for *Renaissance* also meant for Erasmus a rebirth of Christian antiquity. That restoration of pristine Christianity necessitated, as a first step, the preparation of editions of the patrists. He therefore edited an impressive number of them, among them Cyprian, Hilary, Ambrose, Augustine, Lactantius, Basil, and Jerome (nine volumes), granting them the same unquestioned authority that other Humanists had bestowed on pagan authors. It also meant a return to the Greek New Testament and a challenge to the so-called Vulgate, Jerome's Latin version, which had enjoyed unchallenged prestige throughout the Middle Ages.

Drawing on his vast knowledge of Greek and using the best manuscripts available to him, Erasmus published in 1516 the *Novum Instrumentum* containing the purified Greek text of the New Testament, notes, as well as a Latin translation which deviated markedly from the Vulgate. Hailed as "the greatest scholarly achievement of German Humanism" and as "a landmark in the history of Biblical scholarship,"[18] its importance is fourfold: (1) for all its defects, the edition, for the first time, made accessible to all interested scholars the New Testament in its original language. Improvements and emendations could be made now in reference to a widely available text. (2) In applying the philological method of textual criticism to a book that so far had been considered sacrosanct, Erasmus raised questions and created an awareness of the relationship between the original, the translation and interpretation. (3) For German literature, Erasmus's Greek edition has special significance since Luther used it for his masterly translation of the New Testament (1522). (4) Finally, the publication of this edition assured Erasmus the place of an undisputed authority for the scholarly study of the Bible in Europe.

If Erasmus provided the tool for a more critical analysis of a part of the Scriptures with his *Novum Instrumentum,* he gave us in his *Enchiridion Militis Christiani* [Handbook of a militant Christian written 1501, published 1503] insights into his religious thinking.[19] The genesis of this manual is worth telling in brief. While he was staying with a friend in Tournheim, he was asked by a certain Mrs. Poppenruyter to reform her good-for-nothing husband, Johann, an arms manufacturer from Nuremberg, who with profitable impartiality supplied the emperor and his enemies alike with weapons. Granting this request, Erasmus dedicated his *Enchiridion* to Poppenruyter who thus became the unlikely recipient of this Latin work. In keeping with Poppenruyter's quasi-military profession, the Humanist chose the name *Enchiridion,* which in Greek means both "handbook" and "dagger." The arms manufacturer in turn presented his scholarly friend with a real dagger. As Bainton dryly remarks, "Neither made any use of the weapon of the other."[20]

Even though Johann Poppenruyter profited little by this handbook, many other people apparently did, for after its reprinting in 1518 it became one of the most popular books in Europe and had a strong influence upon "Zwingli, Bucer, the Spiritualists, Anabaptists, Spanish mystics and the savants of Enlightenment."[21] Ideas that Erasmus reiterated throughout his life are developed here in programmatic form. He maintained, for instance, like Mutianus, that true piety consists not in the faithful observance of religious ceremonies but rather in a spiritual inwardness and the imitation of Christ. According to him, the "military service" of a Christian should consist primarily of the inner, spiritual fight of man against his own passions and his victory over his longing for material goods. Humility, tenderness, love—these are the virtues of a true Christian. One can understand why the study of the Gospel was of such central importance to Erasmus but also why the author of this booklet was regarded with considerable suspicion in some quarters of the Church, for his emphasis on the spiritual side of religion coupled with sharp attacks on monasticism and the mechanical performance of lifeless rituals could be interpreted as a plea for the abolition of the external apparatus of the Church.

While studying in Paris between 1495 and 1499 Erasmus partly supported himself by tutoring young men, writing for them simple conversations designed to improve their fluency in Latin. Initially these exercises were extremely simple, not to say primitive, and not much different from the awkward first dialogues in a modern text-book for elementary French, German, or Spanish. Gradually, however, as the students progressed in their linguistic studies, these model conversations became not only longer but also more entertaining. For almost twenty years, they circulated in manuscript among his numerous friends and acquaintances until they were published, without his consent, in 1519, by the German Humanist Beatus Rhenanus (Johann Froben in Basel). Angered by this unauthorized publication, Erasmus himself prepared a new and expanded version in 1522. Between that year and 1533 at least twelve new editions came out, and one hundred reprints appeared before his death.[22] This success was not limited to the sixteenth century. In many schools the *Colloquies* became a textbook; the Pilgrims brought it to America, and in the seventeenth century every Harvard student was expected to be familiar with these dialogues.[23]

The appeal to the reader, including the modern one (for the *Colloquies* have lost nothing of their freshness), lies, first of all, in their language. No one north of the Alps could write a livelier, wittier, and more refined Latin than Erasmus. There is a lightness and vivacity in these sketches and little dramas that are unmatched. But their interest also lies in the topics themselves. In these dialogues the great Humanist had found a flexible medium for commenting on and criticizing current issues, ideas, institutions, and individuals. Though Erasmus spared no one, he reserved his sharpest arrows for the monks, religious abuses, the credulity of the people, and the worship of relics. In "A Pilgrimage for Religion's Sake," for instance, he makes fun of relic worship: at a famous shrine in England, where the milk of Mary is exhibited and worshipped, two skeptical visitors wonder why the blessed Virgin could leave so much milk: "It's scarcely credible a woman with only one child could have so much, even if the child had drunk none of it," one pilgrim says, whereupon his friend adds, "The same thing is said about the Lord's cross, which is exhibited publicly and privately in so many places that if the fragments were joined together they'd seem a full load for a freighter. And yet the Lord carried his whole cross" (68). In "The Funeral" Erasmus mocks the undignified squabbling between the members of the various mendicant orders, while in "Charon" he accuses the friars of inciting wars, saying that their motives are really very selfish: "They make more profit from the dying than from the living. There are wills, masses for kinsmen, bulls and many other sources of income" (116).

It is not difficult to see why the *Colloquies* enjoyed their greatest success in the years following the beginning of the Reformation. Understandably Erasmus's attacks on the failings of monks and friars and on superstition and ignorance did not sit well with Catholics. Well aware of that circumstance, he has one of his characters say, with a charming touch of self-deprecating humor: "Kings make wars, priests are zealous and increase their wealth, theologians invent syllogisms, monks roam through the world, the commons riot, Erasmus writes colloquies. In short, no calamity is lacking" (128). Although the orthodox theologians could not prevent this latter calamity altogether, they at least tried to reduce its effect. In 1526 the Theological Faculty of the University of Paris censured the *Colloquies,* describing their author as a "pagan" who "mocked at the Christian religion and its sacred rites and customs" (xxvi), and when the Index of Forbidden Books was established the *Colloquies* were of course included.

Crossing the Alps on horseback from his extended stay in Italy in the summer of 1509, Erasmus conceived of the idea of a praise of folly. Upon his return to England he wrote down the work within a few days, dedicating it to his friend Thomas More, in whose house he was staying, not without good-naturedly teasing the famous Englishman with a pun on his name, for the Greek title, *Moriae Encomium,* is an allusion to More's name. The work, published in 1511, became a huge success and was translated into the various European languages. In the course of the centuries it went through six hundred editions.

The basic literary device is simple enough: from a pulpit and in front of an audience of faithful followers Lady Folly delivers a praise, or encomium, of herself. Following ancient models, she first describes her origins as the daughter of Plutus (Wealth) and the nymph Neotes (Youthfulness) and then introduces her attendants: Self-love, Flattery, Forgetfulness, Laziness, Pleasure, Madness, Luxury, Rowdiness, and Sound Sleep. With the aid of these companions Folly dominates the entire world. According to her, the very origin and continuation of the human race is due to folly, for would any man submit to the yoke of matrimony if he considered first, like a wise man, the pros and cons of marriage. Or, conversely, would any woman yield to the advances of a man if she knew about the pains of childbirth and the difficulties of raising children? Marriage itself would not be possible without the partners constantly deceiving each other through flattery or deception. The same is true of friendship. It too depends on flattery and not seeing or not wanting to see one's friend's faults. Just as flattery is a deception of others, self-love is a deception of oneself. But without that, no branch of human learning was ever discovered, for it is self-love or thirst for glory that motivates human beings to think up and hand down to posterity so many extraordinary things.

Yet self-love is also a source of happiness, Folly continues. People of all walks of life are not only sustained by their delusions of their own importance, they are actually happy in their role. And a role we all play: "Now the whole life of mortal men, what is it but a sort of play, in which various persons make their entrances in various costumes and each one plays his own part until the director gives him his cue to leave the stage."[24] We are, Folly argues, like the people in Plato's cave, gazing in wonder at the shadows and images of the real things. Our very happiness depends on our ability to be deceived and deluded, and the least miserable among men are those who approach the intelligence level of brute animals while the wise men with their ability to see behind the veil of illusions are the unhappiest. Fortunately they are a rare lot: "You can see what would happen if men everywhere were wise: we would need another batch of clay, another potter like Prometheus" (47f.).

These, then, are in brief the themes of the first part of Dame Folly's declamation: flattery, deception, self-love are the vital forces that keep the fabric of society intact and sustain the individual human beings in their happiness. These are, of course, very contemporary themes, and one has only to think of the plays by Samuel Beckett or Jean Genet to see the universality of Erasmus's ideas.

While this first part, then, is essentially a description of the general human condition, the second part focuses on specific professions and social classes. It is a variation of the medieval *Ständesatire* ("satire of social classes"), with the difference, however, that more attention is given to those who hold responsible positions in state and church. The list of those coming under attack is long and nobody is spared: grammarians, poets, lawyers, philosphers, courtiers, theologians, princes, kings, monks, bishops, cardinals, and even popes. It is in this part of the book, however, that the perspective of Folly's speech changes. Stepping out of her role of praising herself and those human beings so richly endowed with her gifts, she directly attacks certain professions. Again the theologians, the monks, and the various members of the church hierarchy are subjected most mercilessly to her mordant satire. Hurling scorn at the petty quibbles of Scholastic theologians and the pomp and ostentation of the bishops and cardinals, she contrasts them with the simplicity of Christ and his apostles.

In a curious twist, this simplicity or "folly" is made the theme of the third part of Lady Folly's address. No longer the vital force as in the first part, Folly or foolish behavior is now defined as acting against one's own selfish interests, to throw away possessions, ignore injuries and to love one's neighbor, in other words, act against all the normal human responses. When Erasmus therefore says, ". . . to put it in a nutshell, it seems to me that the Christian religion, taken altogether has a certain affinity with some sort of folly and has little or nothing to do with wisdom" (132), he is not making fun of Christianity but is pointing to the Sermon on the Mount as the central Christian belief.

Erasmus's *Praise of Folly* was not without its antecedents and models. Lucian, for instance, had written an encomium in which the tyrant Phalaris had praised himself. Similarly Aristophanes had composed a mock-praise on poverty. The fool at court was a well-established institution during the Middle Ages, and so was the Feast of Fools. The Germans celebrated "Karneval" and there was, of course, Sebastian Brant's *Narrenschiff*. All this was probably familiar to Erasmus. Moreover, he had just finished the vastly expanded edition of the *Adagia* so that he had almost the entire literature of the Greeks and Romans at his fingertips. To assimilate all that knowledge and still give *The Praise of Folly* an elegant, effortless, and airy touch—that was Erasmus's great accomplishment.

Understandably, not everyone was enthusiastic about this work with its sharp attacks on ecclesiastical abuses. Sharing the same fortunes as the *Colloquies,* it was officially condemned in 1543 by the Theological Faculty of the University of Paris, a fate Madam Folly had predicted herself: "As for the theologians, perhaps it would be better to pass them over in silence . . . For they might rise up en masse and march in ranks against me with six hundred conclusions and force me to recant. And if I should refuse, they would immediately shout heretic. For this is the thunderbolt they always keep ready at a moment's notice to terrify anyone to whom they are not very favorably inclined" (87).

When the little-known Augustinian monk Martin Luther posted his ninety-five theses against the sale of indulgences on the doors of the Castle Church in Wittenberg, neither he nor any of his contemporaries could foresee the far-reaching consequences of that action which eventually resulted in the schism of the Church. For Erasmus the Reformation became a deep personal tragedy. Accused by the Catholics of having "laid the egg that Luther hatched" and by the Lutherans of failing to support their leader, he tried to steer a middle course, attempting in vain to mediate between the two parties.

There were good reasons for the Lutherans to believe that he would champion their cause. Both his persistent criticism of clerical abuses and his emphasis on inward piety as opposed to the mechanical observance of religious ceremonies were in harmony with Luther's demands for a reform of the Church. No wonder, then, that Erasmus was at the beginning perceived by the Lutherans as an ally, so that Albrecht Dürer, one of the Reformer's early followers, exclaimed in 1521, when Luther was believed to have been killed (when in fact he had been spirited away to the Wartburg): "O God! is Luther dead? Who will henceforth so clearly set forth the Gospel to us? . . . Oh! Erasmus of Rotterdam, where art thou? . . . Hear, thou champion of Christ! Ride forth by the side of the Lord Christ; defend the truth; gain the martyr's crown!"[25] But the champion of Christ did not ride forth, nor had he any inclination to gain the martyr's crown. Though initially not without sympathy for the Lutherans, he became increasingly distressed by their intransigence and intolerance. Repeatedly pressured by the Catholics to take a firm stand against them, Erasmus finally yielded, writing not a polemical attack but a well-reasoned treatise, entitled *De libero ar-*

bitrio [On free will, 1524]. In it he attacked Luther's conception that man's salvation depended solely on God's grace, while he himself saw it in a combination of God's grace and good works. Luther, in turn, in his tract *De servo arbitrio* [On the enslaved will, 1525] thanked his opponent for going to the heart of the theological matter instead of wasting his time on such trivialities as purgatory, papacy, and indulgences. To nobody's surprise he restated and actually sharpened his well-known position.

It is one of the ironies of Erasmus's situation that, while he was clearly disassociating himself from the Lutheran position, he was writing at the very same time (in his *Colloquies*) some of the sharpest satires on the worship of saints, pilgrimages, indulgences, and monks. It was evident that he had not given up hope yet for a reform *within* the Catholic Church.

His last years were spent in bitterness. In Basel, where he had been living since 1521, he witnessed the burning of statues, the destruction of pictures, and the abolishment of the mass by the Protestants. Fearing for his life, frail and unable to travel long distances, he moved to nearby Freiburg which had remained Catholic. After his return to a somewhat quieter Basel in 1535, he learned of the execution of his two dear English friends, John Fisher and Thomas More, for their refusal to recognize the king as the supreme head of the Anglican Church.

The man who had believed in reason, tolerance, and consensus saw the beginning of an age marked by irrationality, intolerance, and discord.

Ulrich von Hutten

No greater contrast can be imagined than that between Erasmus of Rotterdam and Ulrich von Hutten. To the extent that Erasmus was diplomatic and often evasive, Hutten was forthright and outspoken. Whereas the Dutch Humanist shunned action and involvement in political affairs, Hutten thirsted for it. While Erasmus was imbued with the spirit of cosmopolitanism, Hutten was possessed by a fierce and militant patriotism. For Erasmus, issues always seemed complicated, for Hutten clear and unequivocal. Erasmus was peace-loving, Hutten combative. In the second part of the *Letters of Obscure Men,* which Hutten is believed to have written (cf. p. 83), he playfully referred to himself as "an arrant brute who once declared that if the Preaching Friars insulted him as they have Johann Reuchlin he would lop off the nose of every monk he met."[26] That was Ulrich von Hutten.

Born in 1488 in Castle Steckelberg near the town of Schlüchtern, Hutten came from an old Franconian family of knights. In spite of the many frictions he had with his relatives, he was extremely proud of his lineage, and it is significant that he was one of the few German Humanists who did not latinize his name. Life in a castle was far less appealing in those days than nineteenth-century Romantics often suggested. In a letter to Pirckheimer (1518) he has given a very graphic description of its hardships: "May the castle be situated on a mountain or in the plain, it is not built for a pleasant stay but for protection, surrounded with a moat and a wall, confined, made even more restricted by the stables for the cows. . . . Everywhere there is the smell of powder, stench of dogs and their droppings . . . . Our ears are subjected to the bleating of sheep, the lowing of cows, the barking of dogs, the shouting of people working in the fields, the rumbling and creaking of wagons and carriages."[27]

When he was only eleven, Hutten was sent to the ancient monastery of Fulda, from which he fled, however, six years later, in 1505, possibly aided by his older friend Crotus Rubeanus. In the the ensuing period he restlessly moved from one university to the next, leading the life of a wandering scholar. Cologne, Erfurt, Frankfurt on the Oder, and Leipzig marked the stages of his academic wanderlust. In Erfurt he was introduced by Rubeanus to Mutianus, who was impressed by Hutten's enthusiasm and wit but at the same time felt uncomfortable with his impetuous temperament. In Frankfurt Hutten received a bachelor's degree. In 1509 he went to Greifswald in northeast Germany, three miles from the Baltic Sea. Poor and destitute—after his flight from Fulda his father had cut off his allowance—he found lodging in the house of the family of Professor Henning Lötze. He was clothed and also given financial assistance. But soon the amiable relationship changed: the personalities of the self-confident professor of jurisprudence and the bellicose poet clashed, and Hutten secretly left the university town in the bitter cold days of December, 1509. On the way, however, servants of Lötze robbed him of all his belongings, including his warm winter coat and, worse still, an unprinted manuscript of his own poetry. Half-naked, he managed to reach Rostock where local professors tried to make amends for the shabby behavior of their colleague at the neighboring university.

The incident would be of only marginal interest in an account primarily concerned with literature had it not provided the stimulus for Hutten's earliest poetic work, the *Querelarum libri duo* [Two books of complaints] (2:19–93), in which the indignant young poet vented his fury in twenty elegies, ten in each book. In a language (Latin of course) vibrating with passion and anger, Hutten described not only the unjust treatment he had received at the hands of the Lötze family but also raised his personal affair to the level of a metaphor of the conflict between the outdated academic establishment and the guild of young poets.

In 1511 Hutten moved to Vienna. Though his stay there, as almost everywhere, was brief, it marked an important turning point in his intellectual development. Inspired by the encounter with Emperor Maximilian and the patriotic Viennese Humanists, he turned from partly personal, partly literary interests to political matters. As a result, he was henceforth more concerned with the alleged injury inflicted on the empire than with personal wrongs suffered, such as in the Lötze affair.

Hutten could not have considered himself a genuine disciple of Humanism, if he had not gone, like so many predecessors and colleagues, to the homeland of Humanism, Italy. There was, however, another incentive for crossing the Alps. Having given up hope for an ecclesiastical career for his son, Hutten's father was willing to finance his legal studies at one of Italy's famed universities. Yet before Ulrich could devote himself to these intellectual pursuits, he became personally involved in the chaotic political and military affairs of northern Italy. Suspected of being an imperial agent, he was imprisoned by the French who were defending Pavia against the Swiss. Fearing for his life and taking no chances on the appearance of future poetic talent to sing his praises, the twenty-four-year-old Hutten composed his own epitaph:

> Born in wretched conditions, leading an anguishing life,
> often suffering ill, both on the water and land.
> Here he lies, Ulrich von Hutten, not deserving such fate,
> killed by the French with their swords,
> innocent although he was. (3:225)

Fortunately, the occasion to use this inscription on his tomb did not arise at this time. Pavia was abandoned by the French and occupied by the Swiss, who in turn suspected him of having sided with the enemy. Thus, instead of being slain by a French sword, as he had feared, he was only robbed and mistreated by the Swiss. Such adventures did not deter Hutten from joining the war for a time as a soldier. The literary fruit of these experiences was a book of Latin epigrams addressed to Maximilian (3:205–68). In it he tells of victories and defeats and the concluding and breaking of pacts and agreements. The majority of the poems is directed against the French. Other targets are the martial Pope Julius II and the Venetians, whose alleged godlessness and perfidy Hutten never tires of castigating. Not the traditional proud lion but the lowly frog should be the heraldic animal of that republic, he declares, convinced at the same time that Venice would eventually be crushed by the empire, whose symbol is the eagle:

> Lately a shameless old frog, coming out of the morass of Venice,
>   sat on the dry ground and croaked, "This is my very own land."
> Jupiter's bird, the proud eagle, from his lofty height quickly
>   descended
>   grabbed him with his sharp claws and tossed the frog back
>   in the swamp. (2:216)

Hutten's Italian stay also opened his eyes to the discrepancy between the spiritual claims of the papacy and its actual power. At that time his criticism of the Roman Curia, which was to reach its highest pitch during the Reformation years, was heard for the first time, as in this poem on Julius II and the sale of indulgences:

> How this huckster of a pope, Julius, swindles all the faithful believers,
>   Offering heaven for sale! He does not possess it himself!
> Sell me whatever you have. Aren't you ashamed, though, to peddle
>   things that you, Julius, own not yourself. (2:266)

To the great disappointment of his family Hutten returned home without an academic degree (1513). Questioned by a third party, how to address the returned son, one of his relatives facetiously suggested a *nemo*, a nobody. The cool reception at home and this cutting remark probably prompted him to write a lengthy poem called *Outis* or "Nobody."[28] In the first part of that work a number

of incredible things are said about Nobody: Nobody was here before
the creation of the world; Nobody is immortal; Nobody is free of
mistakes; Nobody is wise in love, and so on. Gradually it becomes
clear, however, that Nobody is not a creature of fable but that
Hutten uses this device to speak negatively abouth human nature.
Alternating his tone between irony, humor, and satire, he also voices
contemporary concerns as when he says: Nobody unites all the Germans, Nobody dares to criticize the luxury and leisure of the Pope,
Nobody fights the Turks. The charm of the poem, then, lies in its
ambiguity. It is by no means possible to mechanically reverse these
statements to arrive at what Hutten wants to say, and often we have
to take these declarations at their face value. The second part of the
poem deals, more traditionally, with Nobody as the standard excuse
of servants: whenever a culprit is sought, Nobody has done it.
Nobody in this sense is of course a stock figure in popular literature.

In his dedicatory letter to Crotus Rubeanus Hutten declared that
he himself was a Nobody who had no need of recognition and
applause. Hutten will forgive us if we summon the figure of the
poem for a last time and say, "Nobody will believe that!" On the
contrary, he was, like most Humanists with the exception of Mutianus, very much in need of praise and approbation. For the moment, however, it was Hutten's turn to do the applauding. The
object of his praise was the young Archbishop of Mainz, Albrecht
of Brandenburg, to whose court Hutten had attached himself and
whose festive entrance into Mainz the young Humanist felt obligated
to celebrate in a panegyric of 1,300 hexameters (3:353–400). This
ecomium is, in part, put into the mouth of Father Rhine who has
donned his most magnificent coat for the occasion. Woven into this
garment are not only pictures of nymphs but also scenes from German history, which the patriot Hutten enjoys describing in detail.

The remuneration for this literary effort was truly princely. Hutten received two hundred guilders—an enormous sum if we remember that Celtis was first awarded only eight guilders and later
twenty for a much better work. But then the city of Nuremberg
could not sell indulgences to finance her *literati*.

If flattery had guided Hutten's pen in the former case, indignation
and fury directed it in his speeches against Duke Ulrich of Württemberg who had murdered the poet's cousin Hans von Hutten in
order to have the victim's wife for himself. The Hutten clan immediately demanded the head of the culprit, and Ulrich, who a few

years before had been a "Nobody" to his family, was enlisted as the family spokesman to mobilize public opinion. In four addresses, which appeared between 1515 and 1519 (5:1–96), he mercilessly lashed out against his opponent: "He is no longer a prince, a nobleman, a German, a Christian! Indeed he is no longer a human being. For morals and conduct, not physical appearance, constitute man. He has taken off his humanity and put on savagery, cruelty, and inhumanity. From man he has nothing more than his face, and even that is so terrible and fierce that it cannot be considered human. The rest he shares with the wildest beast."[29]

If in these speeches, which were crafted according to all the rules of classical rhetoric, Cicero was looking over Hutten's shoulder, it was Lucian, the neo-Greek satirist, who stood model for his dialogue *Phalarismus* (4:1–24). In this conversation Duke Ulrich of Württemberg, who is only referred to as the tyrant of Swabia, descends into the underworld where he meets Phalaris of Agrigent, who was considered the greatest tyrant of antiquity. Impressed by the duke's story of his murderous deeds, Phalaris gladly yields this honor to his German counterpart. The two despots then reveal their own cruelty by sharing some secrets of the various methods of tormenting people. The Sicilian tyrant, for instance, relates his own favorite torture of locking up people in a hollow ox made of brass and then kindling a fire under the artificial animal. The agonized bellowing coming from the inside delightfully resembles the real bellowing of oxen, Phalaris boasts. It is the Swabian tyrant's turn to be impressed. On the title page of this work Hutten used for the first time his motto "Iacta est alea" ("The die has been cast"), which he later translated as "Ich hab's gewagt" ("I have dared it")—a far cry from Mutianus's "Beata Tranquillitas."

After a second stay in Italy (1515–1517), where his father had sent him still hoping that Ulrich would obtain a law degree, he returned once more to Germany. Here, thirty years after Celtis and seventy-five after Enea Silvio had received these honors, Hutten was crowned poet laureate by Emperor Maximilian. At that time, he once again entered the service of the Archbishop of Mainz and thus received a firsthand knowledge of courtly life. As on so many other occasions, Hutten transformed this experience into literature, a dialogue on the court called *Aula* (4:43–74). Pirckheimer, who was the recipient of this work, answered in a friendly way but advised him not to waste too much time at the court, suggesting instead that he devote himself to scholarly studies. Hutten's reply was a long personal letter (1:195–217). "What other option do I have," he asks, answering his own question and giving his friend the graphic and realistic description of the life of a German knight quoted at the beginning of this section. While he, Hutten, has to live in a drafty castle, disgusted by the stench and noise of animals, in constant fear of enemy attacks, Pirckheimer, he declares, can enjoy the comfort of a well-protected city. But the differences between the two men go beyond different social classes. Rather, they point to dissimilar temperaments. Hutten wanted to get involved with people and events. His best works are therefore those that resulted from personal engagement. Pirckheimer, on the other hand, regarded his participation in the government of Nuremberg as an annoying disturbance of his really important occupation, the study of the Classics. Consequently, Hutten may be considered the more typical representative of his time, the Renaissance, which after all was an era of great discoveries, inventions, explorations, and a tremendous expansion in trade. There was a great zest for life. And it is certainly no accident that at the end of his letter Hutten exclaims: "Oh century! Oh letters! It is a joy to be alive! It is not yet time to lapse into repose, Willibald. Studies thrive and minds flourish! Woe to you barbarism! Accept the noose, look forward to exile" (217).

During his two visits to Italy Hutten had received firsthand impressions of the Roman Curia which were reinforced after his return to Germany. He was not only incensed by the immorality of the priests and the greedy benefice-hunting of the clergy but also by the sale of indulgences and the enormous power of the papacy. He was especially angry that these abuses were directed against his homeland. The literary genre he adopted for his increasingly sharp attacks against Rome was from now on the dialogue. It is in this form, which he had borrowed from Lucian, that his greatest contribution to German literature lies. The importance of the dialogue, which Hutten thus introduced and in his German dialogues later popularized so that they became the primary propaganda weapon of the reformers, can hardly be overestimated.

A group of four Latin dialogues opened his attack: *Febris Primus* and *Febris Secundus* [The first and second fever, 1519], *Vadiscus sive Trias Romana* [Vadiscus or the Roman trinity, 1520], and *Inspicientes* [The onlookers, 1520]. The participants in the first two conversations are the Fever, a personification of the sickness of the time, and the author himself (4:27–41; 101–144). Fever turns to Hutten, who rejects the undesirable guest, but tries to find another home for it. Since the illness insists on a wealthy man, the Humanist recommends Cardinal Cajetan, who is in Augsburg on the occasion of the Imperial Diet of 1518. The Fever, however, declines this offer since Cajetan, disdaining German food, has become too skinny. Hutten's suggestion of a visit to the rich Fugger family is also declined because these wealthy bankers can afford too many competent doctors. Nor can the Fever be persuaded to go to the monks. Eventually, however, a home is found for Febris: it is a pleasure-loving canon.

In the second dialogue the Fever once again asks Hutten for shelter. Though the German Humanist again brusquely rejects this request, the Fever succeeds in drawing him into a conversation about the wild orgies and luxurious life of the canon and more generally about the "perverted life of the clergy." Hutten remains unyielding. But he is so impressed by the Fever's remarks that, out of concern for the German nation, he decides to turn to King Charles for help in calling back the clergy to their proper duties.

The immorality of the clergy also plays a prominent role in the *Vadiscus* (4:145–261). It is not only the longest but also the most important of the four dialogues, containing the most detailed and blistering attacks on Rome. Hutten's work has been called the "declaration of feud with Rome, the great manifesto of his campaign for German liberty."[30] It was, in fact, the gauntlet Hutten threw down to the ecclesiastical hierarchy. In this work he informs his friend Ernolt about what another friend, named Vadiscus, has just told him upon his return from Rome. This Vadiscus, who never actually makes an appearance in the dialogue, has the peculiarity of presenting his Roman observations in groups of three. "There are three things everyone desires in Rome: short masses, old gold, and a lecherous life." Or: "There are three things pilgrims bring back from Rome: an impure conscience, bad stomachs, and empty purses." Or: "Three things are held high in Rome: beautiful women, handsome horses, and papal bulls." Although Hutten subjects all aspects of the Roman hierarchy to his attacks, the main thrust of his criticism is directed against Rome's shameless financial manipulation and exploitation of Germany.

The exhaustive list of grievances contained in this work is impressive and its passion admirable. Moreover, as a document of the

Reformation the *Vadiscus* is certainly interesting. Viewed as a work
of art, however, it must be considered a failure. Since there is no
real exchange of opinions, dramatic quality is lacking. Similarly,
the long inventory of observations, always presented in the same
triadic form, quickly becomes tiring.

Much more effective as literature is the last dialogue of the group,
the *Inspicientes* (4:269–308). The "spectators" or disputants in this
case are the ancient sun god, Sol, and his son Phaeton, the chariot
driver. Giving their horses an opportunity to catch their breath,
they observe, from their divine perspective in the heavens, the events
taking place at the Diet of Augsburg. What they see does not please
them. Cardinal Cajetan, for instance, is shown as accumulating
money for himself while pretending to gain approval of a tax for
the war against the Turks. In addition to the predictable castigation
of the clergy, various social classes are taken to task. The Germans
as a people are also accused of drinking too much. Under these
circumstances it is probably not much of a consolation that the
French are accused of being arrogant, the Spanish of being thieves,
and the Italians of being swindlers. At the end, Cajetan himself
joins in the conversation with the gods. Used to Italy's blue sky,
he angrily accuses Sol of not having shone for ten days—a not
infrequent behavior of the sun god in Germanic latitudes—and
threatens to excommunicate him. The latter tries to mollify the
legate by maliciously remarking that he did not shine brighter
because he knew that Cajetan was doing some things the Germans
were not supposed to see. The cardinal becomes even more furious
when he discovers that Phaeton sides with the Germans in their
condemnation of Roman exploitation. "You accursed man!" Cajetan
shouts, "you criminal, evil doer, son of Satan. How dare you bark
back? Is it a crime for a shepherd to shear his sheep?" Whereupon
Phaeton answers: "It is not a crime if he shears them because good
shepherds do this too. But they don't torment and kill them. You
may say to your Pope Leo that unless he sends a more moderate
legate, he will see a conspiracy of the sheep against an unjust,
unkind, and bloodthirsty shepherd." (4:307).

In order to bring about this "conspiracy of the sheep" Hutten
had to mobilize the masses; he could do this only in the language
they understood—German, as he said in these famous verses:

I used to write in Latin

> which not everyone could understand.
> Now I write for the fatherland,
> for the German people, in their tongue,
> to shout out these things with all my lung. (3:484)

It was an important decision for a Humanist. Early Humanists like Wyle, Steinhöwel, and Eyb had used the vernacular in their translations from Latin. But their works were totally unpolitical. Of the older Humanists, only Sebastian Brant had published the *Narrenschiff* in German, but his aim was not to mobilize the masses but to confront them with their own follies. Other representatives of the *studia humanitatis* had displayed much patriotic sentiment and even praised German occasionally without using it.

Hutten's first German work appeared in September, 1520, under the cumbersome title *Clag vnd vormanung gegen dem übermässigen vnchristlichen gewalt des Bapsts zu Rom, vnd der vngeistlichen geistlichen* [A remonstrance and warning against the presumptuous un-Christian power of the bishop of Rome and the unspiritual spiritual estate, 3:473–526]. Notwithstanding its rhymed form, it is a speech, more emotional than logical, full of passion, warmth, and urgency. Considering that German as a literary language was in its infancy, and that the only meter commonly used was the short-winded *Knittelvers,* Hutten, as a newcomer to this medium, handled the language very well. In addition to listing the well-known grievances against Rome, he skillfully uses his Roman experiences, as when he describes the splendid procession of the Pope who is followed by an endless train of hangers-on. And who pays for all that, Hutten asks? We Germans, of course, with

> our sweat and blood, a sorry sight.
> Should we endure that? Is that right?
> No penny should they get from us
> henceforth, so that they starve to death
> and suffer pangs of neediness,
> lest against our God and name
> such useless people keep up their game. (3:494)

Hutten's second pamphlet, this time in prose, appeared a few months later under the title "A Brief Disclosure of How the Roman Bishops or Popes Have Always Acted against the German Emperors" (5:363–95). It is an historical survey of the relationship between

Popes and German emperors. The result of Hutten's hardly impartial examination is, not too surprisingly, that no Roman pontiff, at any time, did anything beneficial to the German rulers, but always betrayed, deceived, and mistreated them. Ironically, Pope Pius II, the former Enea Silvio, who had played such an important role in the transmission of Humanism to Germany and who, through his *Germania,* indirectly contributed to the development of a German national consciousness, comes in for special criticism.

In addition to influencing public opinion through his works, Hutten took an active political part in the shaping of history during these decisive years of the Reformation. In 1520, for instance, he journeyed to the Netherlands to win over Archduke Ferdinand to his reform ideas. A year later he observed the Diet of Worms from the Ebernburg, the castle of his friend Franz von Sickingen, and noticed with satisfaction Luther's refusal to recant. From here he bombarded the assembly with invectives against the two papal nuncios Aleander and Caracciolo.

It was during that time that he became convinced that force was needed to shake off the "Roman yoke." Everything he did henceforth was intended to prepare the public for such a violent campaign against the *Pfaffen,* the clergy. In short order there followed the *Gesprächbüchlein* [Book of conversations], a translation of his previous Latin dialogues, the venomous attacks on the papal nuncios just mentioned, and a series of four new dialogues, the *Dialogi Novi* [New dialogues]. Paradoxically, these dialogues, written at a period when the vernacular would have been essential for mobilizing and manipulating public opinion, were again composed in Latin. They consist of *Bulla vel Bullicida* [The bull or the bull-killer], *Monitor Primus* and *Monitor Secundus* [The first and second warner] and *Praedones* [The robbers].[31] From the point of view of pure drama, *Bulla vel Bullicida* is the most successful of these conversations. The initial scuffle between the "Papal Bull" and "German Freedom" is described so graphically that one forgets that they are only personifications of abstract ideas. In the beginning of this playlet Freedom calls for help. Onto the stage rushes none other than Ulrich von Hutten, the valorous bull-killer. His services, however, are not needed because, after more dramatic action and much talk, the bull (Latin: *bulla*) bursts by itself like a bubble (Latin: also *bulla*) emitting indulgences, superstition, avarice, hypocrisy, perjury, lechery, and other assorted vices in addition to the expected infernal stench.

The two middle dialogues, *Monitor Primus* and *Monitor Secundus,* are less dramatic. In restrained speech and counterspeech, the warners try to challenge Luther and Franz von Sickingen. The special target of the fourth conversation, *Praedones,* are the German cities that Hutten tried to win over for his plans. This dialogue begins with a fight between a townsman and a knight and ends with their conciliatory handshake.

Yet the desired collaboration between the German cities and the knights described in this work was to remain fiction. Hutten's patriotism was clearly the driving force behind all his actions, whether political or literary. This can be observed from his earliest admonishments and poems to Maximilian to these last dialogues written shortly before his death. Nowhere is it more obvious than in his dialogue *Arminius,* which only appeared posthumously (4:407–18). When Hutten became acquainted with Tacitus's *Annals* in Italy, he discovered in them the figure of the Cheruscan prince Arminius, or Hermann, under whose command the Germans inflicted a humiliating defeat on the Romans in the Teutoburg Forest in A.D. 9, destroying three Roman legions. In Hutten's work Arminius seeks due recognition for his military achievements before Minos, the ancient judge of the underworld. The German leader wishes to be included in the ranks of famous generals in world history, an honor which so far has been accorded only to Alexander the Great, Scipio the Older, and Hannibal. Although Minos is convinced that the highest place should indeed be given to Arminius, tradition can not be changed. Minos, however, is generous enough to grant Arminius a place of honor as the defender of the fatherland.

With this dialogue Hutten elevated the Germanic leader to a symbol of the German character as he saw it: brave, strong, yielding to no one. Invoking the glorious past, Hutten hoped that his contemporaries would settle accounts with Rome in the same way Arminius had done fifteen hundred years earlier. The work found a wide echo in Germany, not only during the Reformation but also in later centuries, and Arminius became the subject of more than ninety novels, plays, and operas.[32] In 1875, four years after the long-desired unification of Germany, a gigantic statue 180 feet tall was erected for Hermann in the Teutoburg Forest. Reflecting the different political circumstances at the end of the nineteenth century, the Cheruscan prince, with raised sword, fiercely looks to the West—to the then "arch-enemy," France.

Just as Arminius had captivated the imagination of poets and playwrights as a valiant fighter for German freedom, his discoverer, Ulrich von Hutten, fascinated German poets like Wieland, Herder, Goethe, and countless others.[33] The most moving of these tributes to Hutten's genius is a cycle of poems called *Huttens letzte Tage* [Hutten's last days] by the Swiss poet Conrad Ferdinand Meyer. In this great lyrical monologue the dying Hutten, who had contracted syphilis in his youth and was only thirty-five when he died in 1523, sees his entire turbulent life pass by in feverish dreams. Recollections of the great figures of his age in art, science, politics, and religion flash across his memory: Dürer, Copernicus, Paracelsus, Dr. Faustus, Erasmus, Zwingli, and Martin Luther. All of these contributed their share to making the early sixteenth century one of the most colorful and intellectually stimulating periods in German cultural history. However, more than any other man of this age, it was Luther who left an indelible imprint on that period, profoundly influencing not only the religious life in Central Europe but also the course that Humanism was to take in Germany.

Chapter Six

Humanism and the Reformation

In 1521, four years after Martin Luther had nailed his ninety-five theses on the door of the Schlosskirche in Wittenberg, setting off the epoch-making event of the Reformation, there appeared a short illustrated pamphlet called *Die göttliche Mühle* [The divine mill]. The woodcut on the title page shows God in the clouds as the owner of the mill; Christ is pouring the grain (i.e., Saint Paul and the Gospels) into the hopper; Erasmus as the miller's man is bagging the flour (strength, faith, hope, and love), and behind him Luther can be seen as the baker who is kneading the bread into dough. The text explains the picture:

> Erasmus of Rotterdam
> has shown to us the proper way
> so that we firmly go, we pray,
> to the Good Book, the evangel,
> which does all other things excel . . .

> Erasmus of his own will
> at once proceeded to the mill,
> so that he may not be behind
> to see about the flour's grind.
> The Holy Gospel's miller man,
> to bag the flour he teaches everyman,
> with his writings does explain,
> so that the flour's sweet taste will remain . . .

> Doctor Luther, an herald of the doctrine true
> has taken it upon himself to bake
> the bread, mixing the flour for our sake.[1]

What is suggested here is that the word of God treated and purified by Erasmus has become the basis of the new Protestant faith. The picture thus expresses what contemporaries took for granted, namely, that there was a causal relationship between the work of Erasmus and that of Luther, or, to express it in more general terms, between Humanism and the Reformation.

The problem of the relationship between these movements is, of course, more complicated than this pamphlet from the beginning of the Reformation implies, and has been a controversial topic among scholars for a long time. Avoiding simplifications, one must ask oneself two sets of questions: First, in what way, if at all, did Humanism prepare the ground for the Reformation? What are the common elements and what are the differences between these two cultural forces? Second, what happened to Humanism after religious struggles had begun to dominate life in Germany? Was it stifled by the Reformation, as some scholars argue, or modified and integrated to serve confessional ends, as other critics maintain? Drawing partially on the material presented in the previous biographical sketches and partially on some new material, we can attempt to answer these questions, although clear-cut answers are virtually impossible to find.

It is not difficult to see why Pirckheimer, Erasmus, Reuchlin, and Hutten were perceived by their contemporaries as forerunners of the Reformation. Each had done his share in exposing abuses of the Church, such as benefice-hunting, misuse of temporal power, as well as the alleged ignorance and immorality of the monks and clergy. Most had also criticized the externalization of piety, demanding a return to an inner religiosity freed from the whole apparatus of institutionalized religion. In addition to criticism of the established Church, Humanists and Reformers shared strong anti-Roman sentiments, albeit for different reasons. The former resented the pretended superiority of the Italians out of national pride, while the latter were outraged by the sameless exploitation of Germany by the Roman Curia. In Hutten these two elements merged.

Historically speaking, both Humanists and Reformers rejected the immediately preceding historical developments as a wrong path, going back instead to a previous period as the true source of inspiration. The Humanists turned to the literature of the Greeks, Romans, and Church fathers; Luther and his followers turned to the Bible. Thus, just as for the champions of the *studia humanitatis* classical antiquity became a norm to be followed, the Holy Scriptures assumed normative character for the Protestants.

In light of these affinities it is not surprising that, at least initially, almost all Humanists enthusiastically supported Luther, often considering his fight against the old ecclesiastical authorities as a continuation of Reuchlin's struggle against the theologians of Cologne.

This was, of course, a profound misunderstanding of Luther's real concerns, which could only last for a limited time. Soon the significant differences between the two movements were bound to emerge. What were these differences?

As a literary and pedagogical movement, Humanism was essentially the achievement of a small number of men who regarded themselves as an élite, an aristocracy not of birth but of the mind, and who used as their medium of communication Latin, the international language of scholarship and learning. The Reformers, on the other hand, increasingly employed the vernacular in order to mobilize the masses for their cause. Hutten's switch from Latin to German exemplifies this tendency most clearly. Moreover, primarily interested in poetry, rhetoric, and philology, the Humanists regarded literature as an autonomous genre, while the Protestants, concerned with the essential question of man's relationship to God, considered its function the dissemination of their religious beliefs.

A decisive rift between Humanists and Reformers occurred when the Reformation threatened to degenerate into open rebellion. Riots in Wittenberg and other cities in 1521/22, the destruction of religious statues and pictures, the open harassment of nuns and monks, and finally the Peasants' War of 1525/26 seemed to demonstrate the disastrous social and political consequences of the Reformation. Afraid that it would destroy not only the social order but also the cultural accomplishments, many Humanists turned away from Luther. As early as 1519 Erasmus had recommended to Luther *civilis modestia* ("civilian modesty") and Mutianus had dryly remarked, "Ego phanaticos lapidatores non amo" ("I don't like these fanatical stone-throwers"). Realizing that the Reformation would only succeed in conjunction with a worldly power, Luther thereupon formed an alliance with the princes, a policy which entailed the virtual elimination of the more radical wing of the Reformation. But even after Luther had come down solidly on the side of the civil authorities with a number of pamphlets including his unequivocal publication "Against the Murderous and Plundering Peasants" (1526) and after

the "plundering peasants," who had tried to improve their wretched
conditions in a desperate uprising, as well as the "fanatical stone-
throwers" had been defeated in a number of brutally one-sided
battles, many Humanists remained skeptical because the differences
concerning the essential theological truths remained.

According to Luther, man could only hope to be saved by God's
grace through his own faith while good works as a way to salvation
were rejected. This belief in the redemption *sola fide*, through faith
alone, was not a minor theological squabble but the cornerstone of
the Lutheran theology. Yet by repudiating the traditional doctrine
of salvation through good works, Luther also rejected Humanist
ideas which stressed man's part in his own redemption. Thus the
very idea of man's perfectibility through the study of ancient literature and culture contrasted sharply with the Reformer's view of
man's essentially sinful nature. Whereas the Humanists had set out
to humanize religion and to make the path to God easier rather
than difficult, Luther deemphasized man's part in the redemptive
process. There is no doubt, then, that in the last analysis, Humanism
in its essence and the evangelical message were incompatible and
that there was no inner affinity "between Luther's religious experience and the efforts of Humanism."[2] The theological differences
between the Protestant Reformation and Humanism are personified
most dramatically by Luther and Erasmus and their exchange of
essays on the free and enslaved will. "You are not pious," Luther
wrote on the margin of his personal copy of the Dutch Humanist's
edition of the New Testament. "You don't have any civility," was
the latter's opinion of the religious Reformer.

The realization of the basic differences between Humanism and
the Reformation, however, does not answer the second question
posed at the beginning of this chapter: What happened to Humanism after the religious strife had begun to dominate intellectual life
in German lands? Various theses concerning this problem have been
advanced. According to a widely held opinion, for instance, the
success of the Reformation actually marked the end of Humanism.
The Germans became so much absorbed by religious issues, so the
theory goes, that typically Humanist concerns like literature and
poetry became irrelevant. One literary historian characterized the
situation as follows: "The muses became silent, theology alone had
the floor."[3] Another critic, coining the phrase of the "Lutheran
pause" argued: "For a generation the German was willing to forego

artistic life because he was completely spellbound by religious matters. The young Humanist buds and sprouts were either nipped completely by the Lutheran movement or had to be bent into the same direction as the Church."[4] This notion of the end of the Humanist movement through the Reformation has been challenged recently by a number of scholars who argue that, far from being stifled by the Reformation, Humanism was integrated into it.[5] To support their theory, they can point not only to the many Humanist works that appeared in the very center of the Reformation, in Wittenberg, during the most active decades of the Reformation,[6] but also to the many dramas, poems, and historical works written by Protestant Humanists in other cities. These Humanists achieved something like a synthesis between the two movements. No other man exemplifies this synthesis more vividly and clearly than Philipp Melanchthon.

Philipp Melanchthon

In terms of importance and impact Philipp Melanchthon has to be ranked with Johannes Reuchlin and Erasmus of Rotterdam. Through his philological, theological, and pedagogical works, through his numerous expert opinions, pamphlets, letters, school syllabi, church statutes, and speeches he had an incalculable influence both on his contemporaries and the following generations. The Protestant Church would be unthinkable without him and so would the German public school system of the sixteenth to eighteenth centuries.

Born in the small village of Bretten near Pforzheim in 1497, Philipp Schwartzert received an excellent grounding in Latin and Greek at an early age, first through private lessons and later in the *Lateinschule* of Pforzheim. The knowledge he acquired here must have sufficiently impressed his great-uncle Reuchlin to change the simple German Schwartzert ("Black Earth") into the much-better-sounding Greek equivalent Melanchthon. At the unusually young age of twelve he was enrolled at the University of Heidelberg, where, it will be recalled, Rudolf Agricola had been the guiding spirit of the Humanists during the 1480s. Though Agricola had died twenty-four years ago, his ideas were still discussed and his works read. In 1511 the precocious scholar Melanchthon received his bachelor of arts degree but was rejected some time later for the master of arts because of his youthful appearance. He therefore transferred to the University of Tübingen, hoping that his boyish looks would not pose a hindrance to the acquisition of scholarly laurels there. That he was already an excellent Greek scholar is documented by a classroom incident from that time. When one of the professors, unable to explain a passage in a Greek text, exclaimed in despair, "Where shall I find a Greek?" the students in unison shouted, "Melanchthon, Melanchthon!"[7] Needless to say, he had no difficulty in obtaining his master's degree in 1514.

One of his first scholarly accomplishments in Tübingen was the edition in verse form of the comedies of Terence. Up to that time these plays had appeared in prose. In 1518, when only twenty-one years old, Melanchthon was appointed professor of Greek at the University of Wittenberg at the recommendation of Reuchlin. In his inaugural lecture entitled "De corrigendis studiis adolescentiae" [On the improvement of studies of young people], he not only gave a detailed diagnosis of the current educational system, but also outlined his own program, which centered—not altogether surprising for a man brought up in the Humanist tradition—on the study of the ancient authors, whom he regarded as the great paradigms of morality. Inculcation of moral values was the principal goal of any education for him, as for many other Humanists.

These ideas, however, were soon to be modified considerably under the influence of Martin Luther, who had been professor of theology in Wittenberg at the time of Melanchthon's arrival. The meeting and subsequent close cooperation with Luther had an important impact not only on Melanchthon himself but also on the entire course of the Protestant Reformation. The first occasion for cooperation between these two men proved to be the Leipzig debate between Luther and Johannes Eck in June, 1519. While Melanchthon did not actively participate in this eighteen-day-long series of disputations, he supplied Luther with a steady stream of fresh arguments, ideas, and memos. So deeply had he soon become involved in Luther's cause that he politely but firmly refused to accept an invitation from his great-uncle Reuchlin to come as a professor to the University of Ingolstadt. The latter, who ironically had lived for a while in Eck's Ingolstadt house, was so irate about his grandnephew's involvement with the Reformation that he not only reneged on his previous promise to bequeath his substantial library to him but also asked him to refrain from any further contacts with him.

About the time this break with Reuchlin occurred, Melanchthon, with Luther's encouragement, turned to the interpretation of Saint Paul's Epistle to the Romans, because the latter's work surpassed, in his view, all other parts of the Holy Scriptures as a source of theological truths. Attempting to distill the main ideas and basic principles (*loci communes*) from this letter, he expanded his work into a synoptic and summary presentation of the views and insights of the Reformers.[8] Polemicizing sharply against Scholastic theology, Melanchthon not only articulated the Protestant ideas of sin, grace, and justification by faith but also clarified the position on the sacraments, saying that only two of them, baptism and the Eucharist, were to be retained by the new church.

The book was enthusiastically welcomed by Luther and his friends. Within four years no fewer than eighteen editions appeared. Melanchthon himself constantly revised it, undertaking major alterations in the 1535 and 1542 editions. Throughout the sixteenth century the *Loci Communes*, as they were called, were considered one of the three foundation pillars of the Reformation. At Cambridge University they became required reading and "Queen Elizabeth I virtually memorized them in order to acquire the foundations of religion together with elegant language and sound doctrine."[9] If the *Loci Communes* were one pillar on which the new church rested, Luther's three pamphlets of 1520 (*On the Babylonian Captivity of the Church*, *Address to the German Nobility*, and *Freedom of a Christian Man*) were the second, and the *Confessio Augustana* [Augsburg confession], written by Melanchthon, was the third.[10]

Composed at the request of those territorial princes who supported Luther to summarize the essential points of the Reformation for the impending Imperial Diet in Augsburg, the *Confessio* was presented to Emperor Charles V on June 25, 1530. It consists of two major parts: the first contains twenty-one articles on major Protestant tenets of faith, such as original sin, justification by faith alone, the ministry, baptism, the Eucharist, confession, free will, and the worship of saints. The second part, written in a more polemical tone, deals with the abuses of the church, celibacy, mass, fasting, monastic vows, as well as the legal power of bishops.

Melanchthon's importance, however, for the young evangelical church lies not only in his writing two of its major theological

documents, but also in his work as an organizer of the school and
university system in Protestant Germany. With an administrative
talent more to be expected from a twentieth-century business manager than a sixteenth-century theologian, he developed new curri-
cula, drafted statutes, worked out procedures for school visitations,
and deeply involved himself in the day-to-day operations of educational life. For forty-two years he delivered numerous speeches,
prepared many expert opinions, and penned ten thousand letters to
various authorities. In Eisleben, Magdeburg, and Nuremberg he
personally took part in setting up the classical school system that
was later adopted by many other cities. He also aided in the establishment of the new universities of Marburg, Königsberg, and Jena
and was asked for assistance in the reorganization of older institutions
including Tübingen, Leipzig, and Heidelberg. To complement his
organizational efforts the hard-working scholar wrote suitable text-
books for students and pupils. In addition to Greek and Latin
grammars, which became standard works, he published numerous
books on virtually all subjects taught at the time. Written in a
lucid style and presented in a logical manner, these works show a
breadth and range of knowledge hardly matched by any man at this
time.

The motives that prompted Melanchthon to devote so much of
his time and energy to the reorganization of education in Protestant
Germany were complex, intertwining personal, historical, and religious reasons. Three can be isolated:

(1) Before coming to Wittenberg in 1518, Melanchthon had been
a scholar who was deeply steeped in the Humanist traditions. Unwilling to abandon this heritage, which he had learned to cherish,
he modified and redirected Humanism. All his life he continued to
read and interpret classical authors.

(2) Melanchthon was therefore deeply shocked when in the early
1520s some of Luther's followers rejected education altogether.
Karlstadt, for instance, his older colleague in Wittenberg, not only
called for a return to the simplicity of primitive Christianity but
also for the abolition of all education, maintaining that Christ and
his disciples had not been learned and that the Lord had not promised
salvation to the educated but to the simple. Discrediting all learning
not only as useless but also as harmful to man's spiritual welfare,
he urged the students to leave the university and learn practical
trades. His calls, and those of like-minded radicals, for an aban-

donment of the studies were answered by many students, who may not always have been guided by the same theological considerations, with the result that some universities fell into a state of total neglect. In 1526 the University of Rostock, for example, had only five students, Erfurt fifteen, and Greifswald was closed altogether from 1526 to 1538. Erasmus's complaint, "Where Lutheranism reigns, knowledge perishes," was echoed by many educated people. It is against this background that we have to view Melanchthon's endeavors at an educational reform. For him, education was an antidote against the barbarism into which he saw his country sliding.

(3) But education was seen not only as an antidote but also as a positive force in the dissemination of the Reformers' ideas. The behavior of Karlstadt, Thomas Müntzer, and others had shown the dangerous implications of a literal interpretation of the principle of the general priesthood, which was one of the basic tenets of the new church, meaning that a priest was no longer necessary as an intermediary between man and God. While not directly challenging this principle, Melanchthon argued that an authoritative interpretation of the Bible could only be undertaken by theologians who were trained not only in the correct Lutheran dogma but also in the reading of Holy Scriptures in the original languages. It was therefore only logical that the study of ancient languages became a key element of all of Melanchthon's educational reforms. That Latin was taught extensively needs no elaboration. It was, after all, the international language of education, administration, and the Church. Greek was included in the curriculum because it was not only the language of great works in philosophy, history, and the sciences but also the idiom of the New Testament, and Hebrew was essential for the study of the Old Testament.

Thus the lights of Humanism burning so brightly in the first two decades of the sixteenth century were not extinguished by the cold blasts of the Reformation, as some critics have argued. Melanchthon's case shows that a synthesis of the two powerful movements was possible. But it is also clear that Humanism was transformed. It was no longer, as it had been for Celtis, for example, an end in itself but had become a tool. "Education was for Philipp the silver bowl carrying the golden fruit of the gospel."[11] At the same time Humanism was by no means a superfluous ornament but had become an indispensable part of his concept of a Christian education. The

Wittenberg reformer placed Humanism at the service of religion but in doing so also preserved it.

Because of his work in education his contemporaries called Melanchthon the "praeceptor Germaniae," the teacher of Germany. Posterity has ungrudgingly conceded him this title.

Joachim Camerarius

In our time the name of Joachim Camerarius has fallen so completely into oblivion that only a few sixteenth-century specialists will be familiar with it. Yet in his own age he was, next to Melanchthon, not only the most important representative of Protestant Humanism but was surpassed only by Erasmus in his scholarly renown and, with the latter's death, was regarded as the leading German Humanist by his peers.[12]

Born in Bamberg as Joachim Kammermeister in 1500, he was sent at age thirteen to Leipzig to receive a thorough grounding in the classical languages. But it was in the Erfurt of Mutianus Rufus and his young friends that he was exposed to the spirit of Humanism. If Erfurt familiarized him with the new learning, it was Wittenberg and his association with Melanchthon that drew him into the orbit of Martin Luther. His splendid academic credentials soon made him a sought-after professor, first at the newly founded *Gymnasium* in Nuremberg (1526–1535), then at the University of Tübingen (1535–1541), and finally of Leipzig (1541–1574).

Like Melanchthon, Camerarius always tried to bridge the widening gap between the confessions. He supported Melanchthon at the Diet of Augsburg in 1530 and also took an active part in the Peace Diet of 1555 in the same city. In 1568 he discussed the possibility of a reunification of the churches with Emperor Maximilian II in Vienna. But then it was too late for reconciliation.

The reputation Camerarius enjoyed all over Europe was well deserved. His productivity was striking. The latest bibliography of his published works lists 183 items.[13] Although his interests were far-ranging, covering virtually all scholarly fields, he was primarily a classical scholar, "one of the most important, if not the most important of Germany in the sixteenth century."[14] In this capacity he edited numerous works by Greek and Roman authors. He reestablished, for instance, the Plautus text that was superior to that of any previous edition so that Scaliger, an eminent philologist himself, admiringly called his colleague "unicum Plauti Aesculapium," a unique doctor of Plautus.

As a translator, he rendered a number of works from Greek into Latin as well as from German into Latin. Honoring a request by his friend Albrecht Dürer, for instance, he translated the latter's treatise *Vier bücher von menschlicher proportion* [Four books on human proportion] into Latin, thus assuring its wide dissemination.

Camerarius's translation of Dürer's work was prefaced by a brief but sensitive biographical sketch of the Nuremberg artist. Later the Humanist could also prove his skill as a biographer in two major *vitae*, one of the Humanist poet Eobanus Hessus, the other of Philipp Melanchthon. While in his profile of Eobanus Hessus he evoked Humanism as it had flourished in Erfurt in the second decade of his century, he was able to describe Melanchthon's life with the intimate knowledge gained during his lifelong association with him. Since the *Vita Melanchthoni* was expanded into an account of the Church and profane history, it has become an invaluable source of information not only on Melanchthon but also about the events the reformer was involved in. Richly interspersed with anecdotes and written in a natural and unpretentious style, its value is only slightly diminished by Camerarius's characteristic tendency to gloss over unpleasant or unfavorable events in Melanchthon's life.

It was, of course, no accident that Camerarius wrote the biography of his slightly older friend, whom he had accompanied on many of his trips. A deep spiritual affinity existed between the two men. Both were conciliatory, shying away from the loud quarrels of the day; both were also profoundly learned and saw Humanism as an indispensable prerequisite for an ethical education. If Melanchthon's position can be summed up by the term of *pietas docta*, learned piety, Camerarius's ideal was the trinity of *pietas*, *virtus*, and *doctrina*; religion, virtue—by which he meant integrity of character, good reputation, and decency—and *doctrina*, Humanist education and erudition.

It was one of the tragedies of Camerarius's life, as it was of German Humanism in general, that these ideals were less and less appreciated. Deeply lamenting the blind fervor of theologians as well as the moral and intellectual decline of the times contributing to the lapse into what he called barbarism and the political disintegration of his native country, Camerarius died in 1574, a bitter and lonely man, long after Humanism had ceased to play the central role it had played during the first twenty years of the sixteenth century.

Chapter Seven
An Appraisal

The impact of Humanism can be seen in four areas: classical scholarship, literature, changes in the intellectual climate, and education.

Classical Scholarship

For all their different personalities and interests, all European Humanists shared a fascination with classical antiquity. Hunting with untiring zeal for manuscripts, they copied, edited, and published them with great care. Such activities required close familiarity with the paleography, orthography, grammar, and syntax of the ancient works. This process of finding lost manuscripts began around 1330 in Italy and was essentially completed by 1530. Through the efforts of the Humanists much of Greco-Latin literature was thus preserved and had these scholars not written a single creative work themselves, they still would be assured an important place in the history of Western thought.

Although the recovery and preservation of Greek and Latin Classics was done by Humanists all over Europe, the Germans contributed a substantial share to this effort. In addition to those works already cited—among them Erasmus's New Testament in Greek, Camerarius's Plautus, and Brant's Virgil and Terence—the labors of such men as Beatus Rhenanus, who edited the Roman historians Velleius Paterculus (first century A.D.), Tacitus, and Livy or Joachim Watt (Vadianus), who produced an exhaustive commentary on the Roman geographer Pomponius Mela (first century A.D.) must be mentioned.

Many German Humanists, it will be recalled, also applied their scholarly acumen to ancient Greek texts, either by editing the originals or by translating them into Latin. Pirckheimer, Reuchlin, Erasmus, and the eminent poet Eobanus Hessus, who not only rendered the *Idylls of Theocritus* but also Homer's entire *Iliad* into Latin verse, distinguished themselves in that area. Further it should be remembered that Reuchlin opened up the world of ancient Hebrew literature through his pioneering studies.

The striving for a better understanding of antiquity was not confined to written works but also included the collection of ancient coins, inscriptions, and artifacts. Thus the Renaissance witnessed not only the birth of classical philology but also the beginnings of classical studies in a wider sense.

Literature

That Humanism significantly changed the physiognomy of German literature has become obvious. In assessing its impact it is useful to distinguish between those works written in Latin and those composed in the vernacular. There is no doubt that the majority of the Humanist works were written in Latin and that these works, such as the *Letters of Obscure Men* and *The Praise of Folly*, have entered world literature. Similarly, it was the Latin version of the *Narrenschiff* that assured its wide dissemination throughout Europe. This does not mean that Humanism had no influence on vernacular literature. Not only the attempts to introduce fresh and modern subject matter into German literature undertaken by the three leading representatives of early Humanism but also the numerous German works that were indirectly patterned after classical models can be mentioned here. Hutten's Reformation dialogues immediately come to mind in this context. Less obvious but perhaps more important is the dependence of the German Baroque poets on neo-Latin poets of the sixteenth century. They clearly saw themselves as successors of a tradition which began with Ovid, Horace, Propertius, and Virgil and was carried on by Celtis, Eobanus Hessus, and other Humanist poets.

This attempt to model vernacular literature on ancient exemplars was by no means limited to Germany. In the thirteenth century Dante in his work *De volgari eloquentia* [On common eloquence] had demanded an Italian poetic language firmly bound to Latin rhetoric and poetics. Similarly, the poets of the French Pleiade shaped their language according to the matrix of the classical languages and literatures with the intention of making it equal and even better. Du Bellay's *Defense et Illustration de la langue française* of 1549, for instance, outlined a program for the enrichment and decoration of the vernacular, suggesting that a polished style should be guided by ancient syntax and rhetoric. In Germany, Martin Opitz in his seminal *Buch von der deutschen Poeterey* [Book of German poetry, 1624] considered it sufficient to refer only briefly to Latin because everything was derived from it anyhow ("weil wir im deutschen hiervon mehr nicht als was die Lateiner zu mercken haben").

Thus, wherever in Europe vernacular literatures began to form, behind them always stood the masterpieces of Greek and Roman literature as models and norms, works that very often had been rescued from oblivion through the labors of the Humanists.

Changes in the Intellectual Climate

A discussion of the impact of Humanism, however, cannot be confined to the relatively narrow field of literature, but must also consider the profound changes of this movement on the intellectual climate of the time.

Partly in reaction to the condescending attitude of the Italians, and partly as the result of a new pride in German achievements, and unwittingly aided by Enea Silvio Piccolomini's *Germania*, a new national consciousness developed in Germany. Its most articulate exponents were Ulrich von Hutten and Conrad Celtis. While Hutten argued for a political and religious renewal, Celtis pleaded for a cultural renovation. In the ensuing centuries this cultural patriotism became all the more pronounced because of the hopelessly fragmented political situation in Germany.

The author in whom the Germans found confirmation of their patriotism was Tacitus, a historian whose works clearly would have been lost had it not been for the antiquarian interests of the Humanists. But there is also no doubt that many ancient authors were not forgotten during the Middle Ages, as the Humanists sometimes claimed. But these writers and their works had indeed been made relative. To justify their reading they had either been interpreted allegorically or regarded, like Virgil's "Fourth Eclogue," as prefigurations of Christianity. Reduced thus to confirm the teachings of the Church, which determined the ideological horizons of the medieval world, their distinct and unique character had been blurred and obscured. All this gradually changed with the emergence of Humanism. By immersing themselves in the authors of ancient Greece and Rome, the Humanists became aware of the existence of another world—a world that was different from the Christian culture of the Middle Ages with its dualism of this life and that of the Beyond and of sin and redemption. They realized that the Christian culture was, after all, not the only valid culture and that there had been a civilization that believed in man's dignity, power, greatness, and perfectibility, ideas that were bound to clash with official Church doctrine.

Having said this, we must immediately caution against the notion that Christianity and antiquity were two unbridgeable cultural forces for the German Humanists. It is true that many representatives of the new learning were openly or, like Mutianus, clandestinely critical of the Church. Others, such as Peter Luder, who once joked that he would believe in a "quaternity" if required to do so, were serenely indifferent to it. Yet, in the final analysis, none of them questioned the essential truths of their Christian heritage but instead sought to reform and enrich it with the values and norms gained through an understanding of ancient pagan culture. This is another reason why most Humanists, at least at the beginning, supported the Reformation, which, after all, was not a call for an abandonment of Christian beliefs but, on the contrary, an appeal for a return to what were perceived to be the true teachings of Jesus Christ.

Education

The German Humanists had a great interest in the theoretical and practical aspects of education. Wimpfeling's works *Isidoneus* and *Adolescentia*, Agricola's *De formando studio* and *De inventione dialectica* as well as the numerous educational writings of Erasmus, Celtis, and Melanchthon should be recalled in this context. It should also be remembered that the universities became the battleground for the fight between Humanism and late medieval Scholasticism. The introduction of the *studia humanitatis* was a difficult process. Sparked by Luder's lectures on the Classics in the late 1450s, it was continued by the establishment of some regular chairs for poetics at various German universities and by Celtis's call for a radical revision of the curriculum in his Ingolstadt inaugural speech, leading to the gradual triumph of Humanism in the first two decades of the sixteenth century. At that time, to use a phrase the historian Peter Gay coined to describe the situation of intellectuals and artists in the Weimar Republic, the former outsiders became the insiders.

The educational reforms of Humanism were not confined to the universities but also extended to the secondary schools. Here the impact was possibly even more far-reaching than on the university level. In the Middle Ages education was largely if not exclusively in the hands of the clergy, which thus had a unique opportunity for perpetuating their ideology. In the fifteenth century tentative attempts were made to break this monopoly. We have seen the difficulties educational reformers like Wimpfeling encountered in their efforts to establish secular schools. But with the growing self-confidence of the southern German cities, church-independent schools were indeed founded, for instance in Nuremberg and Schlettstadt. These remained, however, exceptions. A large-scale diffusion of Humanistic ideas was only possible in conjunction with the Reformation, and it is Philipp Melanchthon, the "praeceptor Germaniae," who deserves credit for this accomplishment.

That Melanchthon's educational reforms met with success was due in large measure to the historical constellation. While opposed by emperor and Pope, the Reformation was supported by a number of territorial princes, who aided Luther not necessarily out of religious convictions but often in the hope of strengthening their own independence with regard to the emperor. Interested in obtaining a well-educated class of loyal and well-trained civil servants, these rulers were willing to provide the financial backing for the establishment of schools and universities, especially since the funding did not come out of their own pockets but mostly from confiscated ecclesiastical property.

Foremost among these Protestant territorial sovereigns (*Fürsten*) were the Electors of Saxony, Frederick the Wise and Moritz, loyal supporters of Luther. In addition to establishing public schools throughout his land, the latter founded the so-called *Fürstenschulen* Grimma, Schulpforta, and Meissen. Producing, in the course of the centuries, a number of remarkable alumni, including Friedrich Gottlieb Klopstock, Gotthold Ephraim Lessing, and Friedrich Nietzsche, these schools and the two universities Wittenberg and Leipzig assured electoral Saxony first place in German education for a long time.

Central to the curriculum were precisely those subjects that the Humanists had advocated, namely, Greek and Latin literature. With one day per week, religious instruction was not exactly neglected but it was also not overemphasized to the point of stifling other subjects. Johannes Sturm, the eminent educational reformer of Strasbourg, summed up the Protestant ideal in the formula of the "sapiens and eloquens pietas," wise and eloquent piety. Each of these elements was to receive equal weight.

Historically, the school system proposed and implemented by men such as Melanchthon and Sturm was a monumental step in the direction of establishing a system that was free from the influence and ideological tutelage of the Church, for the essential and most significant innovation of the Humanist system was, in fact, the separation of education from the monastery, cathedral, or church authority.

While the Protestants thus preserved the Humanist heritage in their territories through the establishment of secular schools, the Catholics went slightly different ways. Here it was a religious order, the newly established Society of Jesus, or Jesuits, who filled the demands for a better education. Different from other orders in that they emphasized the Humanistic cultivation of learning and instruction, the Jesuits assumed the leadership in education in the sixteenth and seventeenth centuries in Catholic lands. In Bavaria, for instance, the supervision of the entire school system was entrusted to them. Although inculcation of religious values was naturally given more weight, it was again essentially the Humanistic curriculum that formed the core of the instruction.

Thus, in spite of the tragic polarization into two religious camps, the Classics-oriented Protestant *gymnasium* modelled on Melanchthon's prototype and its Catholic counterpart introduced by the Jesuits were to constitute a common bond uniting all educated Germans. Although in later centuries many works of the Humanists were forgotten, the heritage of the classical world, as it had been rediscovered and preserved by them and transmitted through the *gymnasium*, was kept alive. With its linguistic, literary and moral values, this legacy of Rome and Greece was to have a profound impact on German intellectual life.

Notes and References

Preface

1. Joël Lefebre and Jean-Claude Margolin, eds., *L'humanisme allemand* (1480–1540). XVIIIe Colloque International de Tours (Munich/Paris, 1979), p. 5 (paraphrase of a much longer quote). Hereafter cited as *L'humanisme allemand*.

Chapter One

1. Lewis W. Spitz, *The Religious Renaissance of the German Humanists* (Cambridge, Mass., 1963), p. 354.
2. Wallace K. Ferguson, "The Interpretation of the Renaissance: Suggestions for a Synthesis," *Journal of the History of Ideas* 12 (1951): 486.
3. Paul Oskar Kristeller, "The Humanist Movement," in *Renaissance Thought* (New York, 1961); 10
4. Augusto Campano, "The Origin of the Word 'Humanist,' " *Journal of the Warburg and Courtauld Institutes* 9 (1946): 60–73.
5. Kristeller, "Humanist Movement," p. 9.
6. Karl Gillert, *Der Briefwechsel des Conradus Mutianus* (Halle, 1890), p. 8.
7. Quoted in Heinz Otto Burger, *Renaissance. Humanismus. Reformation* (Bad Homburg, 1969), p. 17.
8. Pico della Mirandola, *Oration on the Dignity of Man,* trans. A. R. Caponigri (Los Angeles, Chicago, New York: Gateway Editions, 1956), p. 4.

Chapter Two

1. I follow in this interpretation H. O. Burger (cf. note 7 of Chapter One).
2. *Vom Mittelalter zur Reformation. Forschungen zur Geschichte der deutschen Bildung* (Berlin: Weidmann, 1912–39).
3. Paul Joachimsen, "Vom Mittelalter zur Reformation," *Historische Vierteljahrsschrift* 20 (1920–21): 426–70.
4. Georg Voigt, *Enea Silvio de Piccolomini als Papst Pius II und sein Zeitalter* (Berlin: Reimer, 1856–63), 3 vols.
5. *Aeneas Silvius, Germania,* ed. Adolf Schmidt (Cologne, 1962). Schmidt also published a German translation in the same year. A translation into English is being prepared by E. Bernstein.

6. Ibid., p. 9f.

7. Ibid., p. 47f.

8. Ibid., p. 49.

9. Text in Frank E. Baron, "The Beginnings of German Humanism: The Life and Work of the Wandering Humanist Peter Luder," Ph.D. diss., University of California, Berkeley, 1966, p. 208.

10. Text in Wilhelm Wattenbach, "Peter Luder, der erste humanistische Lehrer in Heidelberg," *Zeitschrift für die Geschichte des Oberrheins* 22 (1869): 100–10.

11. Text in Baron, "Beginnings of German Humanism," pp. 207–9.

12. The episode is related in some detail by Baron, p. 121f.

13. Text in Baron, "Beginnings of German Humanism," p. 212f.

14. Ibid., p. 208.

15. Ibid., p. 173.

16. Cf. Heinz Entner, *Frühhumanismus und Schultradition in Leben und Werk des Wanderpoeten Samuel Karoch von Lichtenberg* (East Berlin: Akademie-Verlag, 1968).

17. Niclas von Wyle, *Translationen*, ed. Adelbert von Keller (1861: reprinted, Hildesheim, 1967).

18. Ibid., p. 9.

19. Ibid., p. 7f.

20. Ibid., p. 86.

21. Printed in Max Herrmann, *Albrecht von Eyb und die Frühzeit des deutschen Humanismus* (Berlin: Weidmann, 1893); *Appeal*, pp. 104–7; *Speech in Praise of*, pp. 109–10 (partial text).

22. "Ehebüchlein" in *Albrecht von Eyb, Deutsche Schriften* I, ed. Max Herrmann (Berlin, 1890). First three quotations on p. 8, last quotation on p. 68.

23. *Boccaccio: De claris mulieribus, deutsch übersetzt von Stainhöwel*, ed. Karl Drescher (Tübingen, 1895), p. 215.

24. Ibid., p. 182.

25. Walther Borvitz, *Die Übersetzungstechnik Heinrich Steinhöwels* (Halle: Niemeyer, 1914), p. 129.

Chapter Three

1. The standard works on Wimpfeling are: Charles Schmidt, *Histoire littéraire de l'Alsace à la fin du XVᵉ et au commencement du XVIᵉ siècle* (Paris, 1879), 1:1–188, and Joseph Knepper, *Jakob Wimpfeling (1450–1528) Sein Leben und seine Werke nach den Quellen dargestellt* (Freiburg im Breisgau, 1902).

2. Jakob Wimpfeling, *Stylpho,* trans. and ed. Harry G. Schnur (Stuttgart, 1971). Contains Latin text, German translation, and brief afterword.

3. "Scientia hac tempestate non implet loculos, non universitas, sed Roma remunerare solet." Ibid., p. 20.

4. Jakob Wimpfeling, *Adolescentia,* ed. Otto Herding (Munich: Fink, 1965).

5. Knepper, *Wimpfeling,* p. 125.

6. Latin text and Wimpfeling's own translation into German in Emil von Borries, *Wimpfeling und Murner im Kampf um die ältere Geschichte des Elsasses* (Heidelberg, 1926).

7. This episode and many others of this controversy are described by Schmidt, *Histoire littéraire,* p. 57ff.

8. Ibid., p. 62.

9. Knepper, *Wimpfeling,* p. 289.

10. *The Correspondence of Erasmus,* trans. R. A. B. Mynors and D. F. S. Thomson (Toronto: University of Toronto Press, 1976), 3:23–33.

11. Schmidt, *Histoire littéraire,* p. 96.

12. The most recent treatment of Brant's life and works is Edwin H. Zeydel, *Sebastian Brant* (New York, 1967). Cf. also: Charles Schmidt, *Histoire littéraire* (Paris, 1879), 1:189–333.

13. Zeydel, *Brant,* p. 58; Schmidt, *Histoire littéraire,* p. 230.

14. Translated by author from Schmidt, p. 226.

15. Schmidt, *Histoire littéraire,* 2:340–73.

16. Most of them are reprinted in Sebastian Brant, *Das Narrenschiff,* ed. by Friedrich Zarncke (1854; reprint ed. Hildesheim, 1964).

17. Cf. Sister Mary Alvarita Rajewski, *Sebastian Brant. Studies in Religious Aspects of His Life and Works with Special Reference to the Varia Carmina* (Washington, D.C.: Catholic University of America Press, 1944).

18. Zeydel, *Brant,* p. 69.

19. P. Heitz, ed., *Des Sebastian Brant Flugblätter* (Strasbourg: Heitz and Mündel, 1915).

20. Quoted in Sebastian Brant, *Tugent Spyl,* ed. Hans-Gert Roloff (Berlin: de Gruyter, 1968), pp. 127–29.

21. Dieter Wuttke, *Die Histori Herculis des Nürnberger Humanisten und Freundes der Gebrüder Vischer, Pangratz Bernhaubt gen. Schwenter* (Cologne and Graz: Böhlau, 1964), pp. 222–27.

22. For a detailed description cf. Zeydel, *Brant,* pp. 74–105.

23. From Edwin H. Zeydel, *The Ship of Fools by Sebastian Brant* (New York, 1962), p. 58.

24. Ibid.

25. Zarncke, ed., *Das Narrenschiff,* " . . . dass es nämlich im wesentlichen eine übersetzung und zusammenkitting von stellen aus verschiedenen alten, biblischen und classischen schriftstellern ist."

26. M. O'C. Walshe, *Medieval German Literature: A Survey* (Cambridge, Mass.: Harvard University Press, 1962), p. 288.

27. Ulrich Gaier, *Studien zu Sebastian Brants Narrenschiff* (Tübingen: Niemeyer, 1966) and *Satire. Studien zu Neidhart, Wittenweiler, Brant und zur satirischen Schreibart* (Tübingen: Niemeyer, 1967).

28. Zarncke in *Das Narrenschiff* has excerpts from the Latin, French, English, and Dutch translations, pp. 205–49.

29. "In Italia summus esse poterat, nisi Germaniam praetulisset." In Erasmus, *Dialogus cui titulus est Ciceronianus* (Basel: Froben, 1529) p. 169.

30. A brief summary of his impact can be found in William H. Woodward, *Studies in Education during the Age of the Renaissance* (Cambridge: At the University Press, 1906), pp. 79–81.

31. Brief summary of his life in Franz Joseph Worstbrock, "Rudolf Agricola," *Die deutsche Literatur des Mittelalters,* 2d ed., (Berlin and New York: de Gruyter, 1978), 1: columns 84–93.

32. List of the five vitae in Worstbrock, column 84.

33. Walter J. Ong, *Ramus: Method, and the Decay of Dialogue* (Cambridge, Mass.: Harvard University Press, 1958), p. 96.

34. In Ludwig Bertalot, "Rudolf Agricolas Lobrede auf Petrarca," *La Bibliofilia* 30 (1928): 382–404.

35. "Hic vir studia humanitatis, quae iam extincta erant, reparavit." In Eugenio Garin, ed., *Prosatori latini del Quattrocento* (Milan: R. Ricciardi, 1952), p. 44.

36. In Hans Rupprich, *Humanismus und Renaissance in den deutschen Städten und an den deutschen Universitäten* (1935; reprint ed., Darmstadt, 1964), pp. 164–83.

37. Ibid., p. 165.

38. Ibid., p. 172.

39. Translated into German by Georg Ihm, *Der Humanist Rudolf Agricola* (Paderborn: Schöningh, 1893).

40. For a list of the editions see: Walter Ong, *Ramus and Talon Inventory* (Cambridge, Mass.: Harvard University Press, 1958), pp. 534–58.

41. Spitz, *Religious Renaissance of German Humanists,* p. 28: Ong, *Ramus. Method and the Decay of Dialogue,* p. 100.

42. *De inventione dialectica* (Cologne, 1539), 3:16.

Chapter Four

1. Throughout this section the author is indebted to the following studies on Celtis: Lewis W. Spitz, *Conrad Celtis: The German Arch-Humanist* (Cambridge, Mass., 1957); Spitz, *Religious Renaissance of German Humanists,* pp. 81–109; Leonard Forster, *Selections from Conrad Celtis, 1459–1508* (Cambridge, 1948). An inexhaustible mine of information on Celtis's life

and thinking is his correspondence, Hans Rupprich, *Der Briefwechsel des Konrad Celtis* (Munich, 1934), hereafter cited as *Briefwechsel*.

2. Forster, *Selections*, p. 23.

3. Full title "Ad Apollinem repertorem poetices ut ab Italis ad Germanos veniat." Text in Forster, *Selections*, pp. 20–21.

4. Karl Hartfelder, ed., *Fünf Bücher Epigramme* (Berlin, 1881), p. 32, and Forster, *Selections*, pp. 34–35.

5. Spitz, *Arch-Humanist*, p. 22; *Briefwechsel*, p. 55.

6. *Briefwechsel*, p. 55; English quoted from Spitz, *Arch-Humanist*, p. 23.

7. *Briefwechsel*, p. 286.

8. Spitz, *Arch-Humanist*, p. 60.

9. Modern edition by Felicitas Pindter, *Ludi Scaenici* (Budapest: Egyetemi Nyomda, 1945).

10. Spitz, *Arch-Humanist*, p. 83; Georg Ellinger, *Geschichte der neulateinischen Literatur Deutschlands* (Berlin and Leipzig: de Gruyter, 1929), 1:443: "In ihm und in Hutten erreicht die lyrische Dichtung des Humanismus ihren Höhepunkt."

11. Cf. Eckhard Bernstein, *Die erste deutsche Äneis: Eine Untersuchung von Thomas Murners Äneis-Übersetzung aus dem Jahre 1515* (Meisenheim: Anton Hain, 1974).

12. *Briefwechsel*, p. 495.

13. Ibid., p. 432ff.

14. Latin text and prose translation in Forster, *Selections*, pp. 26–27. Verse translation my own. This poem is actually not from the *Amores* but from the *Odes*.

15. Hartfelder's edition (cf. note 4) is considered out-of-date today. Dieter Wuttke discovered a manuscript in the Landesbibliothek, Kassel, Germany, containing the five books of epigrams as they were apparently intended for printing. Wuttke, "Unbekannte Celtis Epigramme zum Lobe Dürers," *Zeitschrift für Kunstgeschichte* 30 (1967): 321–25.

16. Cf. Jacques Ridé, "Un grand projet patriotique: Germania illustrata," in Lefebre and Margolin, eds., *L'humanisme allemand*, pp. 99–111.

17. Reprinted in Rupprich, *Humanismus und Renaissance*, pp. 286–95.

18. Reprinted in Albert Werminghoff, *Conrad Celtis und sein Buch über Nürnberg* (Freiburg im Breisgau: Herder, 1921).

19. Indispensable for any study of Reuchlin is Ludwig Geiger, *Johann Reuchlin. Sein Leben und seine Werke* (1871; reprint ed., Nieuwkoop, 1964).

20. Ibid., p. 24.

21. Text of *Sergius* in Hugo Holstein, *Johann Reuchlins Komödien* (Halle, 1888), pp. 107–26.

22. Text in Holstein, *Komödien*, pp. 11–34. Also Johannes Reuchlin, *Henno*, trans. and ed. Harry C. Schnur (Stuttgart, 1970).

23. Ernst Beutler, *Forschhungen und Texte zur frühhumanistischen Komödie*, Mitteilungen aus der Hamburger Staats-und Universitäts-Bibliothek, N. F., vol. 2 (Hamburg: Selbstverlag der Staats-und Universitätsbibliothek, 1927) esp. pp. 105–48.

24. Geiger, *Reuchlin*, p. 27.

25. Modern reprint: *De rudimentis hebraicis libri* 3 (Hildesheim and New York: G. Olms, 1974).

26. Leo Rosten, *The Joys of Yiddish* (New York: Pocket Books, 1970), p. 60. Cf. the pioneering study by Gershom G. Scholem, *Major Trends in Jewish Mysticism* (New York: Schocken, 1961). Also, Joseph Leon Blau, *The Christian Interpretation of the Cabala in the Renaissance* (New York: Columbia University Press, 1944) and Spitz, *Religious Renaissance of German Humanists*, pp. 61–80.

27. Charles G. Nauert, *Agrippa and the Crisis of Renaissance Thought* (Urbana: University of Illinois Press, 1965), pp. 134–35.

28. Blau, *Christian Interpretation*, p. 41.

29. Geiger, *Reuchlin*, pp. 205–454.

30. German translation in modern edition: Johannes Reuchlin, *Gutachten über das jüdische Schrifttum*, ed. and trans. Antonie Leinz von Dessauer, Pforzheimer Reuchlin Schriften, vol. 2 (Konstanz: Thorbecke, 1965).

31. Dessauer, *Gutachten*, p. 33.

32. E. Böcking, ed., *Epistolae obscurorum virorum* in Ulrich von Hutten, *Opera*, supps. 1 and 2 (1864–1869; reprint ed. Osnabrück: Otto Zeller, 1966), a critical edition with contemporary documents. Francis G. Stokes, ed. and trans., *Epistolae obscurorum virorum* (New Haven: Yale University Press, 1909). Text and English translation. Ulrich von Hutten *et al.*, *On the Eve of the Reformation. Letters of Obscure Men*. Introduction by Hajo Holborn (New York: Harper and Row, 1964). Hereafter the letters will be cited in text as Eov *(Epistolae obscurorum virorum)*, I or II referring to the first or second part, followed by number of the letter. The translations are my own.

33. Walther Brecht, *Die Verfasser der Epistolae Obscurorum Virorum*, Quellen und Forschungen zur Sprach-und Culturgeschichte der germanischen Völker, vol. 93 (Strasbourg: Trübner, 1904) and Aloys Bömer, ed. Epistolae obscurorum virorum, vol. 1, Introduction; vol. 2, Text. (1924; reprint ed., Aalen: Scientia Velag, 1978).

34. Stokes, *Epistolae*, p. 1.

35. Ibid., p. liv.

Chapter Five

1. The letters are collected in Carl Krause, *Der Briefwechsel des Mutianus Rufus* (Kassel, 1885) and Karl Gillert, *Der Briefwechsel des Conradus Mu-*

tianus, 2 vols. (Halle, 1890). References to these two editions will be made in the text.

2. The copper engraving is frequently reproduced. Among many others in Spitz, *Religious Renaissance of German Humanists,* facing p. 165.

3. Indispensable for a study of Pirckheimer are Willehad P. Eckert and Christoph von Imhoff, *Willibald Pirckheimer: Dürers Freund* (Cologne: Wienand, 1971). Contains not only various articles on the Nuremberg Humanist but also excerpts in German translation of most of his works. For other studies see Bibliography.

4. Cf. George Boas, *The Hieroglyphics of Horapollo* (New York: Pantheon Books, 1950).

5. Karl Rück, *Willibald Pirckheimers Schweizerkrieg* (Munich, 1895).

6. Willibald Pirckheimer, *Opera politica, historica, philologica et epistolica,* ed. Melchior Goldast (1610; reprint. ed. Hildesheim and New York: G. Olms, 1969), p. 82 (my translation).

7. These views are not too far from what has been believed until recently. The newest medical findings were conveniently summed up for the layman in *Newsweek* (June 30, 1980, p. 72). According to this report, overeating cannot cause the disease, but consuming certain foods helps to bring on attacks. The same is true for alcohol. The age-old notion that gout has something to do with the male sex-drive is apparently correct. The disorder does in fact have a curious connection with the male hormone, testosterone.

8. Latin text in Rupprich, *Humanismus und Renaissance,* pp. 116–35. This quotation is from pp. 119–20.

9. Ibid., p. 127.

10. Cf. Karl Giehlow, "Die Hieroglyphenkunde des Humanismus in der Allegorie der Renaissance," *Jahrbuch der Kunsthistorischen Sammlungen des allerhöchsten Kaiserhauses* 32 (1915): 170ff.

11. Reprinted in Rupprich, *Humanismus und Renaissance,* pp. 136–39 (my translation).

12. Text in Arnold E. Berger, *Die Sturmtruppen der Reformation* (Leipzig: Reclam, 1931). English translation and commentary by Thomas W. Best, *Eccius Dedolatus; a Reformation Satire* (Lexington: University Press of Kentucky, 1971).

13. Pirckheimer's role in this affair is very competently sketched by Harold J. Grimm, *Lazarus Spengler. A Lay Leader of the Reformation* (Columbus: Ohio State University Press, 1978), pp. 38–43.

14. Spitz, *Religious Renaissance of German Humanists,* pp. 183–93.

15. Anecdote in Burger, *Renaissance,* p. 217.

16. Told by Roland H. Bainton, *Erasmus of Christendom* (New York, 1969), p. 3.

17. For a detailed analysis of the various editions see Margaret Mann Phillips, *The "Adages" of Erasmus* (Cambridge: At the University Press, 1964).

18. Burger, *Renaissance,* p. 414; Bainton, *Erasmus,* p. 133.

19. English translation, Erasmus, *Handbook of the Militant Christian,* transl. with introduction by John P. Dolan (Notre Dame: Fides Publishers, 1962).

20. Bainton, *Erasmus,* p. 66. Cf. also for genesis of this work Otto Schottenloher, "Erasmus, Johann Poppenruyter und die Entstehung des Enchiridion Militis Christiani," *Archiv für Reformationsgeschichte* 45 (1954): 109–16.

21. Spitz, *Religious Renaissance of German Humanists,* p. 221.

22. All these figures are based on Erasmus, *Ten Colloquies,* transl. with introduction by Craig R. Thompson (New York: Liberal Arts Press, 1957), p. xx. The following translations are Thompson's, page references to which are hereafter cited in text in parentheses.

23. Thompson, p. xxiv.

24. Desiderius Erasmus, *The Praise of Folly,* transl. with an introduction by Clarence H. Miller (New Haven: Yale University Press, 1979), p. 43. Hereafter page references given in the text are to this work.

25. Quoted in Spitz, *Religious Renaissance of German Humanists,* p. 236.

26. Stokes, *Epistolae,* p. 504.

27. *Ulrichi Hutteni Opera,* ed. Eduardus Böcking (1859–70; reprint ed., Aalen: Otto Zeller, 1963), vols. 1–5 and supps. 1 and 2. A masterpiece of nineteenth-century scholarship and a quarry of information on Hutten and his time. Henceforth cited in text with volume number and page number in parentheses. This letter in 1:195ff.

28. Böcking, 3:107–18. Reference is made to Odysseus who taunted the Cyclops by calling himself Nobody.

29. Translation based on David Friedrich Strauss, *Ulrich von Hutten* (Leipzig: Insel, 1914), p. 87f. (First published Leipzig: Brockhaus, 1858).

30. Hajo Holborn, *Ulrich von Hutten and the German Reformation* (New York, 1966), p. 114.

31. Böcking, 4:309–406. Cf. Barbara Könneker, "Vom 'Poeta Laureatus' zum Propagandisten: die Entwicklung Huttens als Schriftsteller in seinen Dialogen von 1518–1521" in *L'humanisme allemand,* pp. 303–19 (cf. note 1 of Preface).

32. Elisabeth Frenzel, *Stoffe der Weltliteratur* (Stuttgart: Kröner, 1963), pp. 53–56.

33. Ibid., pp. 285–87.

Chapter Six

1. Text of this pamphlet in Schade, *Satiren und Pasquillen aus der Reformationszeit* (1863; reprint ed., Hildesheim: Olms, 1966), p. 1926. Quoted and briefly analyzed by Hans-Gert Roloff, "Thomas Naogeorg und das Problem von Humanismus und Reformation" in *L'humanisme allemand,* p. 455.

2. Holborn, *Ulrich von Hutten,* p. 136.

3. Wilhelm Scherer, *Geschichte der deutschen Litteratur,* 10th ed. (Berlin: Weidmann, 1905), p. 275.

4. Wolfgang Stammler, *Von der Mystik zum Barock 1400–1600,* 2d ed. (Stuttgart: Metzler, 1950), p. 303–4.

5. For instance Roloff, see note 1.

6. Harold Jantz, "German Renaissance Literature," *Modern Language Notes* 81 (1966): 410.

7. Anecdote in Clyde L. Manschreck, *Melanchthon: The Quiet Reformer* (New York, 1958), p. 35.

8. Charles L. Hill, trans., *The Loci Communes of Philipp Melanchthon* (Boston: Meador, 1944).

9. Manschreck, *Melanchthon,* p. 83.

10. *Augsburg Confession,* ed. and trans. J. M. Reu (Chicago: Wartburg Publishing House, 1930).

11. The most recent collection of essays on Camerarius is Frank Baron, ed., *Joachim Camerarius (1500–1574). Beiträge zur Geschichte des Humanismus im Zeitalter der Reformation* (Munich, 1978).

12. Baron, *Camerarius,* pp. 233–51.

13. Konrad Bursian, *Geschichte der classischen Philologie in Deutschland* (Munich and Leipzig: Oldenbourg, 1883), p. 186.

14. Sesto Prete, "Camerarius on Plautus," in Baron, *Camerarius,* pp. 223–27.

Selected Bibliography

PRIMARY SOURCES

1. Collection of Texts

Becker, Reinhard P., ed. *German Humanism and Reformation*. New York: The Continuum Publishing Co., 1982. Texts by Johann von Tepl, Sebastian Brant, Erasmus, Conrad Celtis, Martin Luther, Ulrich von Hutten, Crotus Rubeanus, Thomas Müntzer and Sebastian Lotzer.

Heger, Hedwig, ed. *Spätmittelalter, Humanismus, Reformation*. Vol. 1, *Spätmittelalter und Frühhumanismus*. Vol. 2, *Blütezeit des Humanismus und Reformation*. Munich: Beck, 1975, 1978.

Rupprich, Hans, ed. *Die Frühzeit des Humanismus und der Renaissance in Deutschland*. In *Deutsche Literatur in Entwicklungsreihen* (DLE), Reihe Humanismus und Renaissance 1. 1938. Reprint. Darmstadt: Wissenschaftliche Buchgesellschaft, 1964.

―――――, ed. *Humanismus und Renaissance in den deutschen Städten und an den Universitäten*. In DLE, Reihe Humanismus und Renaissance 2. 1935. Reprint. Darmstadt: Wissenschaftliche Buchgesellschaft, 1964.

Schmidt, Josef, ed. *Renaissance, Humanismus, Reformation*. In *Die deutsche Literatur. Ein Abriß in Text und Darstellung*, 3. Stuttgart: Reclam, 1976.

2. Individual Authors

Agricola, Rudolf

Allen, Percy S. "The Letters of Rudolf Agricola." *English Historical Review* 21 (1906): 302ff.

Bertalot, Ludwig. "Rudolf Agricolas Lobrede auf Petrarca." *La Bibliofilia* 30 (1928): 382–404.

"In laudem philosophiae et reliquarum artium." In *Humanismus und Renaissance in den deutschen Städten und an den Universitäten*, edited by Hans Rupprich. Leipzig, 1935. Reprint. Darmstadt: Wissenschaftliche Buchgesellschaft, 1964, pp. 164–83.

Brant, Sebastian

Lemmer, Manfred, ed. *Sebastian Brant. Das Narrenschiff.* Tübingen: Niemeyer, 1962. Latest edition of Brant's text.

Zarncke, Friedrich, ed. *Sebastian Brants Narrenschiff.* Leipzig: Wigand, 1854. Reprint. Hildesheim: Olms, 1964. Excellent edition. Contains also a wealth of other material on Brant.

Zeydel, Edwin H., trans. *The Ship of Fools by Sebastian Brant.* New York: Columbia University Press, 1944. Reprint. New York: Dover Publications, 1962. Very good annotated English translation with all the woodcuts of the original.

Celtis, Conrad

Forster, Leonard. *Selections from Conrad Celtis, 1459–1508.* Cambridge: At the University Press, 1948. Contains major poems and speeches by Celtis, in Latin with English translations.

Hartfelder, Karl, ed. *Fünf Bücher Epigramme.* Berlin: Calvary, 1881.

Pindter, Felicitas, ed. *Quattuor libri amorum, secundum quattuor latera Germaniae.* Leipzig: Teubner, 1934.

———, ed. *Libri odarum quattuor. Liber epodon. Carmen saeculare.* Leipzig: Teubner, 1937.

Rupprich, Hans, ed. *Oratio in gymnasio in Ingelstadio publice recitata.* Leipzig: Teubner, 1932.

———, ed. *Der Briefwechsel des Konrad Celtis.* Munich: Beck, 1934.

Crotus Rubeanus (Epistolae obscurorum virorum)

Böcking, Eduardus, ed. *Epistolae obscurorum virorum* in Ulrichi Hutteni, *Opera,* supps. 1 and 2. 1864–1869; reprint ed. Osnabrück: Otto Zeller, 1966.

Bömer, Alois, ed. *Epistolae obscurorum virorum.* Vol. 1, Introduction; vol. 2, Text. 1924; reprint ed. Aalen: Scientia Verlag, 1978.

Hutten, Ulrich von et al. *On the Eve of the Reformation. Letters of Obscure Men.* Introduction by Hajo Holborn. New York: Harper and Row, 1964.

Stokes, Francis G., ed. and trans. *Epistolae obscurorum virorum.* New Haven: Yale University Press, 1909. Text and English translation.

Erasmus of Rotterdam

Allen, Percy S. et al., eds. *Opus epistolarum Des. Erasmi Roterodami.* 12 vols. Oxford: Clarendon, 1906–1958.

Dolan, John P. *The Essential Erasmus.* New York: New American Library, 1964.

Olin, John C., trans. and ed. *Christian Humanism and the Reformation: Selected Writings of Desiderius Erasmus.* New York: Harper Torchbooks, 1965.

For translations of *The Praise of Folly,* the *Colloquia* and the *Adages* see notes 17, 22, and 24 of Chapter Five.

Eyb, Albrecht von

Eyb, Albrecht von. *Das Ehebüchlein.* Nuremberg: Koberger, 1472. Reprint. Wiesbaden: Pressler, 1966.

Herrmann, Max, ed. *Albrecht von Eyb. Deutsche Schriften.* Berlin: Weidmann, 1890. Contains *Ehebüchlein* and the translations of three plays.

Hutten, Ulrich von

Böcking, Eduardus, ed. *Ulrichi Hutteni Opera.* Vols. 1–4 and Supps. 1–2. Leipzig, 1859–64. Reprint. Aalen, 1963. A mine of information on Hutten and his time.

Mettke, Heinz, ed. *Ulrich von Hutten. Deutsche Schriften.* Leipzig: Bibliographisches Institut, 1972.

Ukena, Peter, ed. *Ulrich von Hutten. Deutsche Schriften.* Munich: Winkler, 1970.

Melanchthon, Philipp

Hill, Charles Leander, trans. *The Loci Communes of Philipp Melanchthon.* Boston: Meador, 1944.

—————, trans. *Selected Writings of Philipp Melanchthon.* Westport, Conn.: Greenwood Press, 1978.

Scheible, Heinz, ed. *Melanchthons Briefwechsel.* Stuttgart/ Bad Cannstatt: Frommann-Holzboog, 1977.

Mutianus Rufus, Conradus

Gillert, Karl, ed. *Der Briefwechsel des Conradus Mutianus.* Halle: Handel, 1890.

Krause, Carl, ed. *Der Briefwechsel des Mutianus Rufus.* Kassel: Freyschmidt, 1885.

Piccolomini, Enea Silvio

Baca, Albert R. ed. and trans. *Selected Letters of Aeneas Silvius Piccolomini.* Northridge, Calif.: San Fernando Valley State College, 1969. English and Latin.

Schmidt, Adolf, ed. *Aeneas Silvius: Germania.* Cologne/ Graz: Böhlau, 1962. In Latin.

Silvio Piccolomini, Enea. *Opera Omnia.* Basel, 1551. Reprint. Hildesheim: Olms, 1965.

Widmer, Berthe, ed. *Enea Silvio Piccolomini, Papst Pius II. Ausgewählte Texte aus seinen Schriften.* Basel: Schwabe, 1960. In Latin and German.

Pirckheimer, Willibald

Goldast, Melchior, ed. *Opera politica, historica, philologica et epistolica.* Frankfurt, 1610. Reprint. Hildesheim: Olms, 1969.

Reicke, Emil, ed. *Willibald Pirckheimers Briefwechsel.* 2 vols. Munich: Beck, 1940, 1956.

Rück, Karl, ed. *Willibald Pirckheimers Schweizerkrieg.* Munich: Verlag der königlichen Akademie, 1895. In Latin.

Reuchlin, Johannes

Benzing, Josef, ed. *Johannes Reuchlins Augenspiegel.* Munich: Froben, 1961.

Geiger, Ludwig, ed. *Johann Reuchlins Briefwechsel.* Tübingen: Litt. Verein Stuttgart, 1875.

Reuchlin, Johann. *De verbo mirifico,* 1494; *De arte cabalistica,* 1517. Reprint. Stuttgart: Frommann, 1964.

————. *De rudimentis hebraicis libri 3,* 1506. Reprint. Hildesheim and New York: G. Olms, 1974.

Schnur, Harry C., ed. and trans. *Henno.* Stuttgart: Reclam, 1970.

Steinhöwel, Heinrich

Drescher, Karl, ed. *Boccaccio: De claris mulieribus, deutsch übersetzt von Stainhöwel.* Bibliothek des Litt. Vereins Stuttgart, 205. Tübingen, 1895.

Hess, Ursula. *Heinrich Steinhöwels 'Griseldis'.* Munich: Beck, 1975. Analysis and modern edition of the "Griseldis."

Österley, Hermann, ed. *Steinhöwels Äsop.* Bibliothek des Litt. Vereins Stuttgart, 117. Tübingen, 1873.

Wimpfeling, Jakob

Borries, Emil von: *Wimpfeling und Murner im Kampf um die ältere Geschichte des Elsasses.* Heidelberg: Winter 1926. Latin text of *Germania* and Wimpfeling's translation into German.

Herding, Otto, ed. *Jakob Wimpfelings Adolescentia.* Munich: Fink, 1965. Excellent introduction to educational ideas of early Humanism.

Schnur, Harry C., ed. and trans. *Jakob Wimpfelings Stylpho.* Stuttgart: Reclam, 1971. Latin-German. Brief afterword.

Wimpfeling, Jakob. *Germania.* Translated and explained by Ernst Martin. Strasbourg: Trübner, 1885.

Wyle, Niclas von

Wyle, Niclas von. *Translationen.* Edited by Adelbert von Keller. Bibliothek des Litt. Vereins Stuttgart, 57. Reprint. Hildesheim: Olms, 1967.

SECONDARY SOURCES

1. General Works

Bernstein, Eckhard. *Die Literatur des deutschen Frühhumanismus.* Stuttgart: Metzler, 1978. Introduction to the lives and works of the major early German Humanists. Almost complete bibliography.

Borchardt, Frank L. *German Antiquity and Renaissance Myth.* Baltimore: Johns Hopkins University Press, 1971.

Burger, Heinz Otto. *Renaissance, Humanismus, Reformation. Deutsche Literatur im europäischen Kontext.* In *Frankfurter Beiträge zur Germanistik,* 7. Bad Homburg: Gehlen, 1969. Very readable treatment of the literature of that period, comparative in scope.

Hoffmeister, Gerhart, ed. *The Renaissance and Reformation in Germany.* New York: Ungar, 1977. Fourteen articles by different authors on some figures of that age. Has some regrettable gaps: there is virtually nothing on Reuchlin, Pirckheimer, Mutianus, and Melanchthon.

Jantz, Harold. "German Renaissance Literature." *Modern Language Notes* 81 (1966): 398–436. Provocative article, argues for a reevaluation of German Renaissance literature.

Joachimsen, Paul. "Frühhumanismus in Schwaben." *Württembergische Vierteljahreshefte für Landesgeschichte.* N.F. 5 (1896): 63–126, 257–288. Seminal for early Humanism.

Junghans, Helmar. "Der Einfluß des Humanismus auf Luthers Entwicklung bis 1518." *Luther Jahrbuch* 37 (1970): 37–101. Excellent.

Kristeller, Paul Oskar. *Renaissance Thought. The Classic, Scholastic and Humanist Strains.* New York: Harper Torchbooks, 1961.

————. *Renaissance Thought II. Papers on Humanism and the Arts.* New York: Harper & Row, 1965. Both books articulate a definition of Humanism that is widely accepted today.

Lefebre, Joël and **Jean-Claude Margolin,** eds. *L'humanisme allemand (1480–1540). XVIIIᵉ Colloque International de Tours.* Munich: Fink/Paris: Vrin, 1979. Thirty-five papers, in French and German, delivered at this congress on German Humanism.

Moeller, Bernd. *Imperial Cities and the Reformation. Three Essays.* Edited and translated by H. C. Erik Midelfort and Mark U. Edwards, Jr. Philadelphia: Fortress Press, 1972. Important; argues that the Humanists and the cities played a decisive role in the spread of the Reformation.

Ritter, Gerhard. "Die geistesgeschichtliche Bedeutung des deutschen Humanismus." *Historische Zeitschrift* 127 (1923): 393–453.

Roloff, Hans-Gert. "Thomas Naogeorg und das Problem von Humanismusund Reformation." In Lefebre and Margolin, eds., *L'humanisme allemand,* pp. 455–75. Argues against the traditional thesis that Humanism was stifled by the Reformation.

Rupprich, Hans. *Die deutsche Literatur vom späten Mittelalter bis zum Barock.* 2 vols. *Geschichte der deutschen Literatur,* part 4. Munich: Beck, 1970– 1973. Rich in facts.

Spitz, Lewis W. *The Religious Renaissance of the German Humanists.* Cambridge: Harvard University Press, 1963. Brilliantly written, very good bibliographical references. Chapters on Agricola, Wimpfeling, Reuchlin, Celtis, Hutten, Mutian, Pirckheimer, Erasmus, and Luther. The best book in English on German Humanism.

————. "The Course of German Humanism." In *Itinerarium Italicum. The Profile of the Italian Renaissance in the Mirror of its European Transformations.* Edited by Heiko A. Oberman with Thomas A. Brady, Jr. Leiden: Brill, 1975, pp. 371–436. Surveys the entire period of German Humanism from the beginnings in Prague to the late sixteenth century.

Stammler, Wolfgang. *Die deutsche Dichtung von der Mystik zum Barock.* 2d ed. Stuttgart: Metzler, 1950.

Voigt, Georg. *Die Wiederbelebung des classischen Alterthums oder das erste Jahrhundert des Humanismus.* 2 vols. Berlin: Riemer, 1859, 1893. Reprint. Berlin: de Gruyter, 1966.

Wuttke, Dieter. *Deutsche Germanistik und Renaissance-Forschung.* Bad Homburg: Gehlen, 1968. Surveys the state of scholarship.

2. Individual Authors

Agricola, Rudolf

Bezold, Friedrich von. *Rudolf Agricola, ein deutscher Vertreter der italienischen Renaissance.* Munich, 1884. Short but important.

Ihm, Georg. *Der Humanist Rudolf Agricola. Sein Leben und seine Schriften.* Paderborn: Schöningh, 1893. Excerpts from Agricola's writings, in German.

Ong, Walter J. *Ramus. Method, and the Decay of Dialogue.* Cambridge: Harvard University Press, 1958. Places Agricola in the development of logic.

Woodward, William H. *Studies in Education during the Age of Renaissance 1400–1600.* Cambridge: At the University Press, 1906, esp. pp. 79–103. Evaluation of Agricola in education.

Brant, Sebastian

Gilbert, William. "Sebastian Brant: Conservative Humanist." *Archiv für Reformationsgeschichte* 46 (1955): 145–67.

Schmidt, Charles. *Histoire littéraire de l'Alsace.* Paris: Sandoz et Fischbacher, 1879, 1:189–333.

Zeydel, Edwin H. *Sebastian Brant.* New York: Twayne Publishers, 1967. First comprehensive study of Brant's life and works.

Camerarius, Joachim

Baron, Frank, ed. *Joachim Camerarius (1500–1574). Beiträge zur Geschichte des Humanismus im Zeitalter der Reformation.* Munich: Fink, 1978. Articles by different authors and a complete bibliography of the primary works.

Celtis, Conrad

Bezold, Friedrich von. "Konrad Celtis, der deutsche Erzhumanist." *Historische Zeitschrift* 49 (1883): 1–45. Reprint, Darmstadt: Wissenschaftliche Buchgesellschaft, 1959. Brief but seminal.

Kemper, Raimund. *Die Redaktion der Epigramme des Celtis.* Kronberg, Taunus: Scriptor, 1975. Polemical, rambling, good bibliography.

Spitz, Lewis W. *Conrad Celtis. The German Arch-Humanist.* Cambridge: Harvard University Press, 1957. Latest biography of Celtis.

Crotus Rubeanus (Epistolae obscurorum virorum)

Brecht, Walther. *Die Verfasser der Epistolae Obscurorum Virorum.* Strasbourg: Trübner, 1904. A detailed treatment of the authorship and literary techniques; still very valuable today.

Erasmus of Rotterdam

Bainton, Roland H. *Erasmus of Christendom.* New York: Scribner, 1969. A masterly study of Erasmus's life and works.

Huizinga, Johan. *Erasmus and the Age of Reformation.* New York: Harper, 1957.

Sowards, Jesse Kelly. *Desiderius Erasmus.* Boston: Twayne Publishers, 1975.

Stupperich, Robert. *Erasmus von Rotterdam und seine Welt.* Berlin and New York: de Gruyter, 1977. The best study in German.

Eyb, Albrecht von

Herrmann, Max. *Albrecht von Eyb und die Frühzeit des deutschen Humanismus.* Berlin: Weidmann, 1893. Unsurpassed study of Eyb.

Hiller, Joseph. *Albrecht von Eyb: Medieval Moralist.* Washington, D.C.: Catholic University of America, 1939. Tries to stress the medieval character of Eyb against Herrmann.

Hutten, Ulrich von

Best, Thomas W. *The Humanist Ulrich von Hutten: A Reappraisal of His Humor.* Chapel Hill: University of North Carolina Press, 1969.

Holborn, Hajo. *Ulrich von Hutten and the German Reformation.* Translated by Roland F. Bainton. New York: Harper Torchbooks, 1966. The best study in English.

Strauss, David Friedrich. *Ulrich von Hutten: His Life and Times.* Translated by G. Sturge. London: Daldy, Isbister and Co., 1874. Classical study by a German liberal who saw in Hutten a fighter for German freedom.

Luder, Peter

Baron, Frank E. "The Beginnings of German Humanism: The Life and Work of the Wandering Humanist Peter Luder." Ph.D. diss., Berkeley, Calif., 1966. Excellent modern study; contains two of the major poems.

Wattenbach, Wilhelm. "Peter Luder, der erste humanistische Lehrer in Heidelberg." *Zeitschrift für die Geschichte des Oberrheins* 22 (1869): 33–127. Pioneering study; contains some of Luder's speeches and letters.

Melanchthon, Philipp

Hartfelder, Karl. *Philipp Melanchthon als Praeceptor Germaniae.* Berlin, 1889: Reprint. Nieuwkoop: de Graaf, 1972. Concentrates on Melanchthon's educational reforms.

Manschreck, Clyde L. *Melanchthon: The Quiet Reformer.* New York: Abingdon Press, 1958. Reprint. Westport, Conn.: Greenwood Press, 1975. A very good study, sympathetic to Melanchthon.

Stupperich, Robert. *Melanchthon. The Enigma of the Reformation.* Translated by R. H. Fischer. London: Lutterworth Press, 1966. Objective.

Mutianus Rufus, Conradus

Halbauer, Fritz. *Mutianus und seine geistesgeschichtliche Stellung.* Leipzig: Teubner, 1929.

Spitz, Lewis W. "The Conflict of Ideals in Mutianus Rufus." *Journal of the Warburg and Courtauld Institutes* 16 (1953): 121–43.

Pirckheimer, Willibald

Markwart, Otto. *Willibald Pirckheimer als Geschichtsschreiber.* Zürich: Meyer and Zeller, 1886.

Reicke, Emil. *Willibald Pirckheimer. Leben, Familie und Persönlichkeit.* Jena: Diederichs, 1930. Popular and short.

Rupprich, Hans. "Willibald Pirckheimer. Beiträge zu einer Wesenserfassung." *Schweizer Beiträge zur allgemeinen Geschichte* 15 (1957): 64–110. Pirckheimer's accomplishments as a translator and philologist.

Reuchlin, Johannes

Geiger, Ludwig. *Johannes Reuchlin. Sein Leben und seine Werke.* Leipzig, 1871: Reprint. Nieuwkoop: de Graaf, 1964. Still the best biography.

Holstein, Hugo. *Johann Reuchlins Komödien: ein Beitrag zur Geschichte des lateinischen Schuldramas.* Halle: Verlag der Buchhandlung des Waisenhauses, 1888.

Krebs, Manfred, ed. *Johannes Reuchlin. Festgabe seiner Vaterstadt zur 500. Wiederkehr seines Geburtstages.* Pforzheim: Selbstverlag der Stadt Pforzheim, 1955. Articles on various subjects concerning Reuchlin.

Steinhöwel, Heinrich

Mück, H.D. "Heinrich Steinhöwel." *Dizionario critico della letteratura tedesca* 2, Turin (1976): 1108–16. Has excellent bibliography.

Wimpfeling, Jakob

Béné, Charles. "L'humanisme de Jakob Wimpfeling." In *Proceedings of the First International Congress of Neo-Latin Studies,* Louvain, Aug. 23–28, 1971. Louvain/Munich, 1973, pp. 77–84.

Knepper, Joseph. *Jakob Wimpfeling (1450–1528). Sein Leben und seine Werke nach den Quellen dargestellt.* Freiburg im Breisgau: Herder, 1902. Detailed study from a Catholic point of view.

Ritter, Gerhard. *Geschichte der Heidelberger Universität,* I. Heidelberg: Winter, 1936. Considers Wimpfeling a crypto-scholastic ("ein verbrämter Scholastiker").

Schmidt, Charles. *Histoire littéraire de l'Alsace.* Paris: Sandoz et Fischbacher, 1879, 1:1–188.

Wyle, Niclas von

Schwenk, Rudolf. *Vorarbeiten zu einer Biographie des Niclas von Wyle und zu einer kritischen Ausgabe seiner ersten Translatze.* Göppinger Arbeiten zur Germanistik, 227. Göppingen: Kümmerle, 1978.

Tisch, J.H. "The Rise of the Novella in Early German Humanism: The Translator Niclas von Wyle (1410–1478)." Australasian Universities Language and Literature Association: Proceedings and Papers of the 12th Congress held at the University of Western Australia, Feb. 1969. Sydney, 1970, pp. 477–99. First treatment of Wyle in English.

Index